DOING THEOLOGY ACROSS CULTURES

MORRIS A. INCH

BAKER BOOK HOUSE
Grand Rapids, Michigan 49506

P9-DUF-541

ISBN: 0-8010-5032-4
Library of Congress Catalog Card Number: 82-71945

Printed in the United States of America

Scripture quotations are from the New American Standard Bible, © The
Lockman Foundation 1960, 1962, 1963, 1968, 1971, 1972, 1973, 1975, 1977.

To

Edward Coray

and the memory of

Evan Welsh

I would have preferred a more extended manuscript to dedicate to Edward Coray and to the memory of Evan Welsh, but circumstances seem to suggest the present one as most appropriate in view of their long-term association with the alumni of Wheaton College, a grant from whom served my interest in ethnotheology some years ago.

Coach Coray, as he is still fondly referred to by many who recall his outstanding leadership in athletics, served as alumni director and subsequently as senior alumni director. Evan Welsh, a beloved former pastor of the College Church in Wheaton, served as chaplain of Wheaton College and later of the Alumni Association. As exemplary servants of Jesus Christ, the lives of these men embody, in my thinking, the finest qualities of Wheaton alumni.

Contents

Preface

Few, if any, concerns should be higher on the Christian agenda than how one is to conceive and express his faith in his cultural setting. It is this subject, sometimes referred to as ethnotheology, which we will consider in this brief work.

In Part One, which deals with general theory, we will explore the concept of revelation as the basis of theological endeavor (chapter 1) and the tension between biblical authority and cultural integrity (chapter 2). The next three parts consist of case studies. We begin in Part Two with biblical case studies: Paul's mission as apostle to the Gentiles (chapter 3) and his admonition to the church at Corinth (chapter 4). In Part Three we turn to three case studies confined to the level of theory: the yin-yang model of thought (chapter 5), an Eastern critique of the Western concept of man (chapter 6), and liberation theology (chapter 7). Part Four details two practical case studies: strategies for relating to a Muslim culture (chapter 8) and to Chinese ancestor worship (chapter 9). All of these case studies illustrate, test, and extend the approach advocated in the opening chapters. Finally, in Part Five we summarize how the Christian faith alters culture (chapter 10).

The reader will discover that the topics are treated in more of a suggestive than exhaustive fashion. He will also find a blend of theory and practice, the general and the particular, the possible and the actual. He will come to appreciate that

7

the subject is not reserved for a theologically elite but relates to all who seek to better understand their faith in their cultural context. Thus this brief study could well be used by adult study groups.

part one

General Theory

Revelation:
The First Issue

To plunge into the subject of the relationship between Christian faith and cultural context without first coming to grips with the issue of revelation is tempting. But to do so would fail to get the broader perspective and impede our progress.

To reveal means to uncover, lay bare, make naked. *Revelation*, then, presupposes that someone or something was hidden, that what was hidden has been disclosed, and that being disclosed it is capable of being understood. Each of these points is an essential component of the idea of revelation.

The Hidden God

In Isaiah 55:8-9 we read:

"For My thoughts are not your thoughts,
Neither are your ways My ways," declares the Lord.
"For as the heavens are higher than the earth,
So are My ways higher than your ways,
And My thoughts than your thoughts."

There is a vast gulf set between God and man, a gulf that resembles the endless expanse of the heavens.

"Now when man's mind begins to concern itself with God, it is baffled," John Stott confesses. "Our minds, wonderfully effective instruments as they are in other realms, cannot immediately help us here. They cannot climb up into the infinite mind of God. There is no ladder. . . . Indeed, the situation would have remained thus, if God had not taken the initiative to remedy it."[1] Stott readily admits the marvel of the human mind. It can investigate the world about us, down to particles invisible to the naked eye and up to the stars many light years distant. It can also reflect on man's distinctive character, so that the psalmist concludes, "I am fearfully and wonderfully made" (Ps. 139:14).

But the mind which operates so well in other regards is baffled when it comes to contemplate the Almighty. Here it falters and fails.

Here also idolatry takes root. Unable to probe the domain of God, we create gods from the stuff available: wood, stone, a fortuitous event, or a human ideal. We exchange "the glory of the incorruptible God for an image in the form of corruptible man and of birds and four-footed animals and crawling creatures" (Rom. 1:23). Man's inability to comprehend God explains the prophet's complaint that "their land has also been filled with idols; they worship the work of their hands, that which their fingers have made" (Isa. 2:8).

We ought rather to let God be God, recognizing that we cannot bring Him down to our proportions. We must allow for His hiddenness or transcendence. We must reject the temptation to turn to idolatry. Stott's words bear repetition: our minds "cannot climb up into the infinite mind of God. There is no ladder."

The Hidden Revealed

Note, however, that Stott's comment does not end there, for he goes on to say: "Indeed, the situation would have remained thus, if God had not taken the initiative to remedy it." *Revelation* is the divine initiative which compensates for what the human capacity lacks. It is the ladder we can climb, the bridge we can cross, the door we can enter.

1. John Stott, *Basic Christianity*, p. 10.

"Revelation consists of the progressive unfolding of God of His character and purposes and mighty acts, in history and through the words of His specially designated spokesmen."[2] It consists in part of God's mighty acts. "Great are the works of the LORD; they are studied by all who delight in them" (Ps. 111:2). We search them out to better understand His ways, to worship Him in truth, and to serve Him faithfully.

Revelation also involves God's interpretation of His acts, an interpretation He provides through select spokesmen. "But know this first of all, that no prophecy of Scripture is a matter of one's own interpretation, for no prophecy was ever made by an act of human will, but men moved by the Holy Spirit spoke from God" (II Peter 1:20–21). Revelation, then, includes the word as well as the works of God.

We read of God's initiative toward man at the dawn of history. "Where are you?" God inquired of Adam and Eve (Gen. 3:9). Following their trespass, they had secreted themselves away. "Where are you?"—the words call to mind the image of hands parting leaves to locate the fugitives.

The Almighty continued His initiative with Adam's posterity. Once, when man's wickedness had grown to an unprecedented degree, God covenanted with Noah to preserve his family from the impending judgment and to allow him to make a fresh beginning thereafter (Gen. 6:18). He wrote the end to one chapter in human history and the introduction to the next. Thus God has continued to reveal Himself to wayward man, formerly through the prophets and in these last days through His Son (Heb. 1:1–2).

Francis Thompson, in his "Hound of Heaven," has given us an unforgettable picture of the Almighty's initiative with man:

> I fled Him, down the nights and down the days;
> I fled Him, down the arches of the years;

2. T. C. Hammond, *In Understanding Be Men*, p. 18.

> I fled Him, down the labyrinthine ways
> Of my own mind; and in the midst of tears
> I hid from Him, and under running laughter. . . .
> Still with unhurrying chase,
> And unperturbed pace,
> Deliberate speed, majestic instancy,
> Come on the following Feet,
> And a Voice above their beat —
> "Naught shelters thee, who wilt not shelter Me."

Man is the hare and God the hound; we hide in a thousand obscure places only to have God flush us out.

The issue is no longer in doubt: the hidden has been revealed. We live in the wake of God's initiative.

The Revealed Understood

God takes up our human language so that we may comprehend His truth, that is, so that what has been revealed may be understood. Kenneth Hamilton makes a telling point: "Because the eternal Word has come in the flesh, we can know that human words are not incapable of expressing divine reality. It is pagan to think that we can do no more than form picture-images of the incomprehensible divine reality."[3] The incarnation has for all time removed the idea of the incomprehensibility of God. To believe otherwise is pagan, not Christian.

Hamilton does not mean, nor should we suppose, that revelation was limited to Christ. In the words of J. Gresham Machen:

> For Jesus Himself plainly recognized the validity of other ways of knowing God, and to reject those other ways is to reject the things that lay at the very centre of Jesus's life. Jesus plainly found God's hand in nature; the lilies of the field revealed to Him the weaving of God. He found God also in

3. Kenneth Hamilton, *Words and the Word*, p. 107.

the moral law; the law written in the hearts of men was God's law, which revealed His righteousness. Finally, Jesus plainly found God revealed in the Scriptures.[4]

Jesus understood (and encouraged us to understand) the revelation found in creation, the moral law, and Holy Writ. What has been revealed is meant to be understood.

We are responsible to act upon what can be understood. "For since the creation of the world His invisible attributes, His eternal power and divine nature, have been clearly seen, being understood through what has been made, so that they are without excuse" (Rom. 1:20). We can perceive God's revelation in creation and so are without excuse; we can witness God's revelation in the moral and religious disposition of man and so are without excuse; we can view God's revelation in the providential course of events and so are without excuse; we can study God's special revelation in Scripture and so are without excuse. God has provided an abundant means whereby we may know of Him and be led to serve Him.

We ought not to leave the question in doubt for a moment. Either man is capable of discovering God by himself or God must choose to reveal Himself if He is to be known. Scripture takes the latter position. The Bible also assures us that God has in fact taken the necessary initiative toward man, so that we may understand His truth, obey His will, and serve His purposes.

We are not left with the impression of man attempting to drag some truth out of the hands of a reluctant deity, but instead the Hound of Heaven pressing after fleeing man. All subsequent discussion will assume the facts of revelation: the hiddenness of God, His initiative in revealing Himself, and therefore our ability to understand what has been revealed and to act upon it.

4. J. Gresham Machen, *Christianity and Liberalism*, p. 55.

What has all this to say about our doing theology in specific cultural settings? It says that God's revelation lies at the heart of our theological endeavor. There are not, strictly speaking, many truths, but one truth viewed from differing perspectives. Christianity is not capable of radical reinterpretation; rather, it is one faith communicated to all mankind. Ignoring the common heritage in the Christian fellowship is as grievous an error as failing to appreciate its rich diversity. Paul's words are meant to be taken with utter seriousness, "But even though we, or an angel from heaven, should preach to you a gospel contrary to that which we have preached to you, let him be accursed" (Gal. 1:8).

The High Road

The topic of this chapter — the tension between biblical authority and cultural integrity — has, if anything, been overworked. It is desirable, however, that we include an abbreviated discussion. The reader who wishes to explore the topic further will find more extended treatments available elsewhere.[1]

A High View of Scripture

In his study of the issue at hand, Donald McGavran wastes no time in presenting a high view of Scripture: "The Bible was written by men in two of the thousands of languages of men, and the words are the words of men. However, since God inspired the authors, the words are at the same time the words of God."[2] A high view of Scripture holds that the Bible is the Word of God in the words of men.

McGavran uses the familiar analogy between the Scriptures and the incarnation of Christ to reinforce the point. As

1. For instance, see Donald A. McGavran, *The Clash Between Christianity and Cultures*, pp. 51–74; Bruce Nicholls, *Contextualization: A Theology of Gospel and Culture*, pp. 37–52; *Let the Earth Hear His Voice*, ed. J. D. Douglas, pp. 3–9, 65–93, 985–1007. Byang H. Kato's polemic *Theological Pitfalls in Africa* accents what is at stake in appealing for a high view of Scripture and culture. Charles Kraft's *Christianity in Culture* illustrates how difficult it is to achieve the ideal: by promoting the integrity of culture, he seems to weaken the case for biblical authority.
2. McGavran, *Clash*, pp. 52–53.

Christ was both God and man, so the Bible is both the Word of God and the words of man. While there may be problems with the analogy, as various writers have pointed out, we dare not lose sight of the both/and nature of Holy Writ. If the Bible were not the words of men, we would have no way to interpret it, and if not the Word of God, we would have no compelling reason to obey it.

In Lewis Carroll's *Through the Looking Glass* Humpty Dumpty boasted, "When I use a word it means what *I* choose it to mean — neither more nor less." Such is the way some seem to approach Scripture, twisting it to meet their presuppositions and preferences. And there is nothing to stop them as long as they assume Humpty Dumpty's license. The only safeguard against taking such flagrant liberties with Scripture is the realization that the Bible is in fact the words of other men delivered in a particular historical context and through a certain literary means. An acquaintance with the historical context and literary means is necessary for proper interpretation. A high view of Scripture recognizes this genuinely human character of the text.

Moreover, unless the Bible is the Word of God we need render it no special consideration. Alice responded to Humpty Dumpty, "The question is whether you *can* make words mean so many different things." Humpty Dumpty replied, "The question is which is to be master — that's all." Yes, that is the question: Which will be master — the Word of God or the perverse will of man to alter reality? Only a high view of Scripture, which acknowledges the Bible as the Word of God, will allow God to rule.

The problems notwithstanding, many persist with a low view of Scripture. "The low view, on the contrary, regards the Bible not as revelation, not as propositional truth, but as a *record* of human insight touched in some vague way by God."[3] It views Scripture as the religious insight of men somehow sponsored by the Almighty.

3. Ibid., p. 55.

There are a number of difficulties with the low view of Scripture, some more obvious than others, but we shall limit our criticism to three. The low view loses hold of the uniqueness of Scripture. Other religious writings appear similarly inspired, edifying, and even authoritative.

For those who maintain that Scripture is unique, the low view runs aground at this point. It reasons that men have recorded whatever they understood of God and that there is truth in all these records. The Bible may be the most effective way of revealing truth, but why that should be or in what regard it is so is difficult to determine. Biblical uniqueness is lost amid the clamor of contradictory truth claims.

The low view also tends to substitute the authority of culture for the authority of Scripture. In order to bring some order out of chaos, it promotes culture as the arbiter of truth.

Thomas J. J. Altizer illustrates both of the problems we have identified and introduces the third. Altizer reflects on his pilgrimage: "Since the summer of 1955 I had been torn between an interior certainty of the death of God in modern history and experience and a largely mute but nevertheless unshakable conviction of the truth of the Christian faith."[4] At first he felt that Christianity might be revitalized by "absorbing the higher and more universal mystical forms of the Orient" — an indication of his difficulty in working out the uniqueness of Scripture. This avenue having failed him, Altizer determined that "our only hope lies in moving through our radically profane consciousness to a new and yet Christian" confession of faith. Altizer insists that denial of the traditional notion of divine transcendence is now a condition for Christian faith and practice. We must allow culture to mandate the nature of our experience. Cultural consensus replaces biblical authority.

Altizer then redefines the meaning of Christ in a world denying divine transcendence. The low view of Scripture sev-

4. Thomas J. J. Altizer, ed., *Toward a New Christianity: Readings in the Death of God Theology*, p. 301.

ers Christ from Scripture in order to discover Him elsewhere. It opts for a Christ of one's own making instead of the historical Christ. It rejects the interpretations of Paul, Peter, and John in favor of some personal preference.

Beware the person who pits Christ against Scripture. He ends up in opposition to both. The low view of Scripture strikes at the heart of the Christian faith — at the person and work of Christ.

The high view of Scripture is necessary if we are to interpret the text accurately, affirm it as divinely authoritative, preserve its uniqueness, resist cultural tyranny, and promote Jesus as Lord. We have no alternative; the low view of Scripture fails at each of these critical points.

A High View of Culture

We couple with a high view of Scripture a high view of culture. "A high view of culture recognizes different ways of thinking and different systems of logic, knowing that these are equally good for conveying meaning — given the circumstance."[5] Some of the factors that determine what is reasonable within a given culture are climate, geography, density of population, and the state of technological progress. When allowed to determine lifestyles in an uninhibited fashion, these factors assure us of a rich diversity among cultures. In a society where writing is unknown, it is *reasonable* to put a high priority on oral transmission. Eating with knife and fork is not a matter of right or wrong, but what is reasonable under the circumstances.

McGavran observes that "Christianity is wholly neutral to the vast majority of cultural components."[6] He takes as an example Nagaland, the easternmost province in India: "At least ninety-five percent of the Naga culture came into the Christian faith automatically." Out of the thousands of com-

5. McGavran, *Clash*, p. 68.
6. Ibid., p. 11.

ponents, perhaps only 5 percent were of any consequence for or affected by the introduction of the Christian faith.

McGavran subdivides this 5 percent into components Christianity encouraged, changed or improved, and prohibited. Some practices seemed to lend themselves to Christian ideals and so were encouraged, the Christians taking the lead among their cultural peers; some practices were altered so as to better express Christian concern; and some practices were prohibited, as with Naga head-hunting. But altogether about 95 percent of the cultural components were left unaffected when Christianity was introduced. This reflects a high view of culture.

At the time of McGavran's writing (1974), more than half of the Nagas had become Christians. Recently, in discussing the fantastic spread of the Christian faith in that sector, a national reported that the figure is now in excess of 80 percent. This is the kind of numerical results one hopes for when the local culture is respected and left intact, that is, when there is a high view of culture.

A low view of culture is not difficult to recognize. It is an ethnocentric perspective which rules out everything not done "our way." It is what gave birth to the image of the "ugly American," but Americans have no monopoly on a low view of culture.

What is wrong with a low view of culture? It rules out the rich diversity of various cultural heritages and in so doing denies the creative expression of man as formed in God's image. A high view of culture is required if man is to carry out God's charge to subdue the earth (Gen. 1:28).

A low view of culture is also wrong in that it fails to appreciate the effect of the fall on every culture — no culture (including our own) is perfect! Man "has known of God's invisible nature and power and deity — and made idols of men and beasts and reptiles. He has known that kindness is better than cruelty — and has been inexpressibly cruel. Consequently, the part God has actually played in cultures has been limited."[7] Not even the best of cultures has escaped the universal results of sin.

Moreover, a low view of culture is ultimately self-defeating. It leads to idolatry of a particular culture, which is a sure road to cultural decay. "It is a humanistic superstition to believe that the man to whom [his own] culture is everything is the true bearer of culture. The opposite is true. Culture necessarily degenerates where it is made God."[8]

On the other hand, a high view of culture will accept the idea that differing cultures represent a variety of reasonable ways of thinking, each of which is determined by its own peculiar set of circumstances. Given a high view of culture, the introduction of Christianity will have a direct effect on only a small minority of the cultural components — whether to encourage, change, or prohibit them. A high view of culture will also see in an individual culture an imperfect response to God's invitation to subdue the earth, and will challenge the effort to deify a particular culture. A high view of culture is not only compatible with but necessarily results from a high view of Scripture.

Concerning Cultural Relevance

What are we to make of the oft-heard insistence that culture is (or should be) relevant to our religion? It all depends on precisely what "cultural relevance" entails. An uncritical appeal for cultural relevance is, in the words quoted earlier from Emil Brunner, "a humanistic superstition." It incorrectly assumes that man is the center of his own existence, history, and creation — none of which is true. It is Christ rather than man that stands at the center.

In the words of Dietrich Bonhoeffer, "Christ is our centre even when he stands on the periphery of our consciousness: he is our centre even when Christian piety is forced to the

7. Ibid., p. 39.
8. Emil Brunner, *Christianity and Civilization*, vol. 1, p. 158.

periphery of our being."[9] Life must be measured by God's standards and that puts Christ center stage whether we perceive Him as being there or not. Bonhoeffer adds that Christ not only stands at the center but He stands there for me. He is the mediator between man and Himself, man and history (as the Messiah), and man and nature. He and He alone can recover for man the true center.

However, we cannot write off the appeal for cultural relevance so easily. There is more to it than we have as yet allowed. It may involve what Bonhoeffer terms "concreteness" — pressing beyond an abstract expression of concern about the world's plight to assist someone in particular with some specific need.

C. S. Lewis well illustrates the point in *The Screwtape Letters*. Uncle Screwtape is lecturing his demonic nephew Wormwood on how to frustrate a new Christian convert: "It is, no doubt, impossible to prevent his praying for his mother, but we have means of rendering the prayers innocuous. Make sure that they are always very 'spiritual,' that he is always concerned with the state of her soul and never with her rheumatism."[10] Screwtape adds that "he will, in some degree, be praying for an imaginary person, and it will be your task to make that imaginary person daily less and less like the real mother."

Prayer proves to be irrelevant when misdirected away from a real person. It becomes squandered on some imaginary individual we have substituted — to the delight of the demonic adversaries.

Prayer also proves irrelevant when it fails to deal with real needs growing out of actual circumstances. It must contend with the pains associated with rheumatism and not some imprecise subject like "the state of her soul." Prayer ought to

9. Dietrich Bonhoeffer, *Christology*, p. 62.
10. C. S. Lewis, *The Screwtape Letters*, p. 16.

touch earth, mentioning someone specific and some definite purpose.

We conclude that the appeal for cultural relevance can be either legitimate or illegitimate. It is legitimate if it entails calling our attention to real persons in actual situations; it is illegitimate if it involves promoting man to the center, a position which only Christ is to hold.

We have refused to pit a high view of Scripture and a high view of culture against one another. A high view of Scripture, properly understood, inevitably includes a high view of culture. Not only is a high view of culture compatible with a high view of Scripture, but any alternative proves self-defeating. A legitimate appeal to cultural relevance is also quite compatible with a high view of Scripture, so that biblical authority and cultural relevance are not competing ideals. They are rather aspects of the same ideal, existing in some sort of creative tension.

Our task would be immeasurably easier were it not for our high regard for Scripture *and* culture. A person could, of course, ignore one or the other and simply promote the alternative he favors. There would be less ambiguity, uncertainty, and tension, but there would also be less integrity, growth, and excitement. The high road (i.e., the high view of both Scripture and culture) may seem more difficult at the moment, but it is certainly more challenging — and it is necessary in any case.

We approach our task with high resolve. We intend to resist the appeal of syncretism, which results from a low view of Scripture; we also mean to withstand what some have called "radical displacement" (the uncritical exchange of one's culture for another), which results from a low view of culture. We see ourselves as holding a course between these two dangers. Not only do we take warning from those who have already fallen prey, but also we give warning to those who even now risk their faith in one direction or the other.

part two

Case Studies: Biblical

3

Paul: Apostle to
the Gentiles

It is reasonable to suppose that the Scripture will provide us with some definite clue as to how to express our faith in a cultural setting. This is not to suggest that the Bible is, or should be understood as being, a scientific textbook on cross-cultural communications, but neither should we ignore the kind of precedent it provides — a rather modest, but not unimportant, paradigm for our own task and ministry.

It is with this in mind that we turn to the first of two paradigms offered by the apostle Paul. When writing to the church at Rome, Paul declared, "Inasmuch then as I am an apostle of Gentiles, I magnify my ministry" (Rom. 11:13). Indeed he did, on this occasion and on others. His declaration reminds us of the monumental task he assumed in crossing cultural barriers, both in word and deed. Our hope is to learn from his experience how we also can best answer God's call.

Paul was bicultural, that is, reasonably at home in two cultures. Though he was a citizen of the Greco-Roman city of Tarsus, he was reared in a devout Jewish home and trained in the rabbinic tradition. The bicultural person is "comfortable and at peace with peoples of diverse styles or norms, while at the same time he is protected from abandonment of his own principles."[1] He at least tolerates and likely appreciates the differences he discovers in the second culture with-

1. Marvin K. Mayers, *Christianity Confronts Culture*, p. 243.

out feeling that he must surrender identity with his primary culture. Thus while Paul relished the idea of being the apostle to the Gentiles, he described himself as "of the nation of Israel, of the tribe of Benjamin, a Hebrew of Hebrews; as to the Law, a Pharisee" (Phil. 3:5).

Paul debated with Peter in this connection: "If you, being a Jew, live like the Gentiles and not like the Jews, how is it that you compel the Gentiles to live like Jews?" (Gal. 2:14). In other words, if you are able to maintain your Jewish identity while accommodating to the Gentile culture, why do you require the Gentiles to abandon their identity in favor of the Jewish culture?

As a matter of fact, Peter had initially been a reluctant convert to the notion that it is possible for one person to combine two cultures. He was troubled by a vision of animals being lowered from heaven and a voice which commanded him to kill and eat (Acts 10:10–20). "By no means, Lord, for I have never eaten anything unholy and unclean," Peter protested. The voice replied, "What God has cleansed, no longer consider unholy." Peter obeyed the Spirit's prompting and went on to minister to the Gentiles gathered at the home of the God-fearing Cornelius.

But Peter's resolve to associate freely with the Gentiles soon wore away under pressure from his Jewish associates. Paul then "opposed him to his face" for holding "himself aloof, fearing the party of the circumcision" (Gal. 2:11–12). Paul persisted in exemplifying the bicultural ideal and urged others to do likewise.

Paul's Teaching Across Cultures

Two of Paul's addresses seem especially helpful for our purpose: his speeches at Lystra (Acts 14:15–17) and at Athens (Acts 17:22–31). Though both audiences were Gentile, one could hardly imagine two such different groups. The Lycaonians "were as yet untouched by the civilized scepticism of society; and the idea of appearances and visits of the gods was quite natural to them as to a genuine pagan peasantry."[2] In contrast, "Athens was still the intellectual and artistic capital of the world."[3] There were the primitive Lycaonians on the one hand and the sophisticated Athenian citizenry on the other, and between them we have virtually the whole sweep of Gentile cultures.

Two emphases characterize the apostle's teaching on these two occasions and a third emphasis appears in Athens. The first has to do with the "living God, who made the heaven and the earth and the sea, and all that is in them" (Acts 14:15). "The God who made the world and all things in it, since He is Lord of heaven and earth, does not dwell in temples made with hands" (Acts 17:24). Nor does any people hold a monopoly on Him.

Paul suggests that God in His providence has brought about cultural diversity, and lingers close to men in their varied cultural settings so that they may turn to and serve Him. Our daily blessings testify to His care and concern for us.

The living God opposes every effort to make any cultural ideal, preference, or aspiration the ultimate. Culture provides the context in which we may encounter the living God; it is the means and not the goal.

The apostle blends in a second theme — "the times of ignorance" (Acts 17:30). "And in the generations gone by He permitted all the nations to go their own ways" (Acts 14:16). Why did God leave man all this time in ignorance? Paul suggests that the times of ignorance had a place in God's purposes, that He did not leave those generations without witness to Him (Acts 14:17), and that they were responsible for the light which they did receive.

God employs culture as a teacher to prepare man for Christ. This seems to be the thrust of Paul's argument. God does not

2. R. B. Rackham, *The Acts of the Apostles*, p. 232.
3. Ibid., p. 301.

hold us responsible for what we have not been taught but for the teaching we choose to ignore.

Paul finally (in Athens) shifts his attention to the advent of Christ: "God is now declaring to men that all everywhere should repent, because He has fixed a day in which He will judge the world in righteousness through a Man whom He has appointed, having furnished proof to all men by raising Him from the dead" (Acts 17:30–31). "The question of the times past is a matter of speculation; S. Paul's concern and ours is with the present and ourselves."[4] Elsewhere, the apostle announced, "Behold, now is 'the acceptable time,' behold, now is 'the day of salvation' " (II Cor. 6:2).

Christ awaits each of us in the future, as Savior or Judge. God attested to this fact by raising Christ from the dead. So Paul believed and so he taught. "If Christ has not been raised, then our preaching is vain, your faith also is vain" (I Cor. 15:14).

Here we discover in brief how Paul confessed his faith across cultures. It remains for us to define the principles involved and to accept Paul's invitation to imitate his ministry (I Cor. 4:16).

Lessons for Today

What can Paul's addresses to the Gentiles teach us about advancing the gospel across cultures? We shall attempt a reply by setting forth five observations.

1. *We may expect a continuity between man's former experience and the Christian message.* Paul notes that in the past the "rains from heaven and fruitful seasons" were a witness to the Gentiles (Acts 14:17). In addition certain of the poets had given them the insight that they were the offspring of God (Acts 17:28). The Athenians attempted to worship God, although they worshiped in ignorance. The vast array of gods testified to the Gentiles' efforts to recognize God's working in the world.

4. Ibid., p. 318.

This continuity in experience suggests that radical displacement will not do as we attempt to spread our theology across cultures. Radical displacement demands that the convert surrender all in his former experience in order to embrace Christ. This approach fails to appreciate the factors God used in preparing the new convert to receive the gospel and their continuing importance in his life.

We learn from social theorists that "in re-socialization the past is reinterpreted to conform to the present reality, with the tendency to retroject into the past various elements that were subjectively available at the time."[5] The task of the convert is to reinterpret his past in the light of his subsequent experience with Christ. He does not drop the past but holds it up in the light of his new-found faith.

This is not to imply that the convert should falsify the former record just because he now discovers that various elements were "subjectively available" in the past. Rather, he understands his past more perfectly because of his present experience with Christ. There was a continuity throughout, even though he did not come to realize this fact until later.

The lesson here is that we should suspect any approach that demands too radical a break with the past. In all likelihood it offers a truncated gospel and restricts the sphere of God's activity.

2. *We may also anticipate a discontinuity between man's previous experience and the good news of Christ.* Paul contrasts the times of preparation and fulfilment, ignorance and knowledge. We pass from B.C. to A.D., the time of the prophets to that of the Son, the "present age" to the age of the Messiah.

This discontinuity in experience means that Christians must reject syncretism. Syncretism surrenders the privileged perspective the convert has gained in Christ. The past, whether

---

5. Peter L. Berger and Thomas Luckmann, *The Social Construction of Reality*, p. 163.

his or someone else's, must not be allowed to assume an importance competitive with the Christian present.

The Christian is not so bold as to suggest that he knows what the future holds, but he does know who holds the future. Helmut Thielicke confesses, "The only thing that matters is the certainty that the fellowship with Jesus Christ to which we have been admitted cannot be broken by anyone or anything — not even by death."[6] We know that we can face and manage the future with Christ. This is "the only thing that matters."

The Christian faith transforms the past. Nothing is ever the same once we have made our way to the cross.

3. *We likewise note that there is an interval between the advent of Christ and the proclamation of the gospel.* The Lycaonians had to wait until the conversion of a zealous persecutor of the church before they were to hear of the advent. The Athenians had to wait until Paul had received a vision at Troas pleading for him to minister on the European continent. Others have waited centuries and still others have yet to hear.

This hiatus has implications for the Christian approach across cultures. Many of our contemporaries resemble the Lycaonians. They are pagan in the sense that they have elevated some aspect of the creation above the Creator. They have not heard or heeded the admonition of the prophets to turn from idolatry to serve the living God. They do not view life from the perspective of Sinai, let alone that of Calvary.

Among Paul's audiences were often found God-fearing Gentiles who had turned from idols to serve the true God. Some of our contemporaries are similarly God-fearing. They are not converts to Judaism, but they do view life from the vantage point of Sinai. There is no Calvary for them.

Then, there are those for whom Calvary is a real event. But even for them, the event may seem removed and difficult

6. Helmut Thielicke, *I Believe: The Christian's Creed*, p. 142.

to comprehend. They may in a sense be post-Christian in their thinking. The truth they have heard no longer seems compelling.

Recognizing that there is an interval between Christ's advent and the proclamation of the gospel and that different audiences are at different stages of knowledge of God, Paul always assumed the perspective of his particular audience, whether Jew or Gentile, when he expressed his faith (I Cor. 9:20). We likewise, when we spread the message for "these last days" (Heb. 1:2), must help men precisely where they are.

4. *We have a responsibility to share the gospel.* Paul witnessed before the Ephesian elders, "I testify to you this day, that I am innocent of the blood of all men. For I did not shrink from declaring to you the whole purpose of God" (Acts 20:26–27). He had faithfully shared with others what he had received from Christ as a sacred trust. He had met his obligation with resolve and determination, and now he could look back with a sense of mission completed.

The Christian is not simply one who comes to Christ but he goes in His name to others. The way of the cross opens up to all the world. The narrow way to life is a broad highway to service.

"For if I preach the gospel, I have nothing to boast of, for I am under compulsion; for woe is me if I do not preach the gospel" (I Cor. 9:16). Sharing the gospel is not some exceptional service but part of the course of the normal Christian life.

5. *We gather that those to whom we speak also have a responsibility.* Paul declares that it is their obligation to seek and grope after God. The Jews who were exiled in Babylon were promised, "You will seek Me and find Me, when you search for Me with all your heart" (Jer. 29:13). A token attempt is not in view here; rather, the desire for God must take precedence over everything else.

The eighth-century prayer of Alcuin reflects the proper

spirit: "O eternal Light, shine into our hearts. O eternal Goodness, deliver us from evil. O eternal Power, be Thou our support. Eternal Wisdom, scatter the darkness of our ignorance. Eternal Pity, have mercy on us. Grant unto us that with all our hearts, and minds, and strength, we may evermore seek Thy face; and finally bring us, in Thine infinite mercy, to Thy holy presence."[7] A man who searches with such resolve will be prepared to honor the will of God once it has been discovered.

To sum up, we have learned from Paul's ministry to the Gentiles that there will be both continuity and discontinuity between a convert's former experience and his Christian life. We have sensed that the people to whom we spread the gospel stand at varied distances from the scene of Calvary. And we have observed the obligation to seek until we find, and having found, to show others the way.

Paul's audiences varied, as do our own, but he always preached as a dying man to perishing men. He was impeded by cultural barriers but pressed ahead. He understood and made adjustments for the cultural diversity which he encountered. He declared, "I have become all things to all men, that I may by all means save some" (I Cor. 9:22). The words and deeds of the apostle to the Gentiles serve as both instruction and inspiration for those who embrace the ongoing task of doing theology across cultures.

7. *Prayers: Ancient and Modern*, p. 13.

4

Paul's Admonition to the Church at Corinth

One of Paul's outstanding ministries was to the thriving city of Corinth. Corinth was one of the largest and most important cities of the Roman Empire at the time. Located on a narrow finger of land that connected the Peloponnesus and northern Greece, the city lay on a crossroads for commerce both north and south as well as east and west. Two seaports, Cenchreae on the Saronic Gulf leading into the Aegean and Lechaeum to the west, served the metropolitan area. Acrocorinth hovered above the city proper, and looking down from the height stood the temple of Aphrodite, attended by a host of sacred prostitutes. With its mixed population and commercial prosperity Corinth gained a reputation for licentiousness. According to one description, at Corinth "all the brutality of the west and all the sensuality of the east met and were rolled into one."[1]

Paul ministered at Corinth for perhaps eighteen months, enjoying success (Acts 18:8) in spite of continuing opposition. Reports that the church was in difficulty reached him after he had taken up residence in Ephesus. The church was characterized by a lack of harmony and partisan squabbles. When Paul received an inquiry from Corinth concerning marriage, meat offered to idols, spiritual gifts, collections for the needy saints, and the projected visit of Apollos, he responded

1. R. D. Shaw, *The Pauline Epistle*, p. 130.

35

not only in regard to these matters but weaved in related concerns of his own.

Eating Meat Offered to Idols

We shall not consider the First Epistle to the Corinthians as a whole. Rather we will concentrate on a portion which shows how Paul related his faith to the cultural pattern of Corinth. Chapter 10 is a directive concerning the eating of meat offered to idols:

1. Participation in the pagan feasts amounted to idolatry and was to be refused under any circumstances.
2. It was permitted to purchase meat from the shops, regardless of whether it had been dedicated to the gods (as would likely be the case).
3. When dining at the home of an unbeliever, Christians were allowed to eat meat, provided that no attention was called to the fact that the meat had been dedicated to idols. Otherwise, they were to refrain from eating, not because the meat had been associated with idols but because eating it might cause offense to others.

Paul provided no categorical answer concerning the eating of meat offered to idols but a range of appropriate responses. Here we see a dynamic model for applying biblical teaching to cultural situations — one which preserves both the authority of Scripture and the integrity of culture. Let us now look more closely at the three points of Paul's directive.

1. Some no doubt argued that Christian liberty allowed them to participate in the pagan feasts. Had they not committed their way to the Lord? Did they not sit in fellowship with His people? What did it matter whether meat were offered to idols or not? But note Paul's answer to the question, Is a thing sacrificed to idols anything, or is an idol anything (v. 19)? "No, but I say that the things which the Gentiles sacrifice, they sacrifice to demons, and not to God; and I do

not want you to become sharers in demons. You cannot drink the cup of the Lord and the cup of demons; you cannot partake of the table of the Lord and the table of demons." Paul is uncompromising in his stand.

There are two elements involved in the apostle's response: the exclusive claim of the Almighty on our devotion and the continuing struggle with the powers of evil. "Do not go after other gods to serve them and to worship them," intoned the prophets (Jer. 25:6). "You shall not worship them or serve them; for I, the LORD your God, am a jealous God, visiting the iniquity of the fathers on the children, on the third and fourth generations of those who hate Me, but showing loving-kindness to thousands, to those who love Me and keep My commandments" (Exod. 20:5–6). One cannot expect God's blessing while courting the favor of Baal or Aphrodite.

Paul likewise affirmed that "our struggle is not against flesh and blood, but against the rulers, against the powers, against the world-forces of this darkness, against the spiritual forces of wickedness in the heavenly places" (Eph. 6:12). We are to "take up the full armor of God" to do battle against the evil principalities in the name of the living God.

The first plank of doing theology within a cultural context is now in place: We must refrain from any practice which compromises our singular allegiance to the Almighty or blunts our attack on the powers of evil. We are as the people of God called to separate ourselves from a sinful and adulterous world and to engage the forces of evil in relentless warfare.

There comes to mind the courageous stand of Korean believers during periods of persecution. Koryo Seminary in Pusan was founded by those who stood firm during difficult days and it still radiates the spirit of its founders. It is in the best tradition of Christian militancy, and as such illustrates what the apostle intended.

2. Paul took a very different approach with regard to meat which found its way into the shops that lined the busy Corinthian streets. Why be concerned over what route it took to

get there? "The earth is the Lord's, and all it contains" (I Cor. 10:26). We should gratefully accept God's provision and partake with a thankful spirit.

There are again two elements behind Paul's thinking: the goodness of God's creation and its availability for man's welfare. We have in the creation account the refrain "and God saw that it was good" (Gen. 1). There is not the slightest hint in Scripture that the earth is other than good.

After the work of creation God said to Adam, "Behold, I have given you every plant yielding seed that is on the surface of all the earth, and every tree which has fruit yielding seed; it shall be food for you; and to every beast of the earth and to every bird of the sky and to every thing that moves on the earth which has life, I have given every green plant for food" (Gen. 1:29–30). The overly scrupulous who disdained the meat offered in shops were in fact rejecting God's gift to them.

Dietrich Bonhoeffer warns that "Christian radicalism, no matter whether it consists in withdrawing from the world or in improving the world, arises from hatred of creation. The radical cannot forgive God His creation."[2] Because the radical hates the world he cannot discover the means to love God; hating the gift, he is unable to love the Giver.

With Bonhoeffer's warning in mind, the second plank in our approach has been set in place: The Christian opts in favor of life and all that enriches it as God's gracious provision. He enters into life with a relish that others covet.

In this connection one is reminded of the late Nigerian churchman Byang Kato. He enjoyed life to its full, even the little things that most overlook, and especially his relations with others and the privilege of service. He also exhibited an infectious sense of humor that eased many a difficult situation. He had taken the apostle's instruction to heart.

3. Paul next depicts a scene at an unbelieving friend's

2. Dietrich Bonhoeffer, *Ethics*, p. 129.

table. The Christian is about to select a piece of meat when warned by a brother sitting nearby that this meat was secured from the temple precinct. What is the Christian to do? The apostle urges, "Do not eat it, for the sake of the one who informed you, and for conscience' sake; I mean not your own conscience, but the other man's" (I Cor. 10:28–29). It is better to forego one's privilege than offend another — whether Jew, Gentile, or Christian.

We must make a distinction between the issue at hand and what Paul addresses elsewhere. Here we are dealing with the weaker brother rather than the seasoned legalist. The weaker brother is one who has not come to appreciate the fuller implications of faith or the legitimate diversity in Christian practice. He is like a tender shoot of grass that can be easily crushed by some inconsiderate act. The legalist has had time to develop his stultifying perspective on life. The former needs to be encouraged and the latter confronted.

The third plank in our approach to culture requires that we be sensitive to the welfare of others. Christian liberty is no substitute for loving constraint.

A More Difficult Issue

Paul turns from his discussion of meat offered to idols to the custom of women being veiled in public, and particularly in the worship service (I Cor. 11:1–6). He explains, "Every woman who has her head uncovered while praying or prophesying, disgraces her head; for she is one and the same with her whose head is shaved." In general, women uncovered their heads as a dramatization of grief or a mark of promiscuity. Paul likely has the latter in mind.

The cultural context is of paramount importance here. Except for periods of mourning, decent women would veil themselves. The gospel has enough problems to contend with without shocking people by breaches of custom. Paul has already warned the Corinthians against giving offense in connection with the eating of meat. Here, in connection with the wearing of the veil, he repeats his concern about giving offense.

Why should the veil have been set aside in the first place? Perhaps to allow the women to speak audibly in the congregation. Apart from such a practical consideration, the issue of freedom would justify raising the question. Are we not at liberty in Christ, whether male or female?

But Paul seems to sense a baser motivation. "If one is inclined to be contentious," he leaves the conclusion to his readers, "we have no other practice, nor have the churches of God." Some delight in sowing discord; the apostle instructs us not to pamper their pernicious ways.

What significance does this teaching have for us whose cultural practices differ substantially from those at Corinth? Shall we require a practice now void of its former implications? Not necessarily. Common sense should tell us as much even if we fail to pick up the gist of Paul's reasoning.

It is significant that the apostle handles this instance in a peculiar fashion — by citing the creation order. He ties into the very nature of man and woman rather than limiting himself to the cultural custom. As a result we are left with a binding principle which may be applied differently from culture to culture.

Paul taught that men and women should be treated with equal respect, as persons created in the image of God and subject to Christ's redemption. But their particular roles are a different matter. God singled out man to assume the leading part, while woman is to exercise a supportive but no less important role. The apostle suggests that God stabilized these positions, not necessarily in regard to specifics but as a principle out of which cultural particulars might legitimately evolve.

To return to the matter of veiling, some churches require a token head covering upon entering the sanctuary. A square of cloth may suffice. This seems a somewhat artless way of keeping Paul's reminder before us, but it is at least a conscientious effort.

Yet the principle has more critical applications. For instance, take the case of a woman who files for divorce because her responsibilities as wife and mother interfere with developing a successful career. She had every right to pursue her career without thought to family responsibilities *until* she spoke her marriage vows, but not thereafter. She has violated her promise to abide by the creation mandate.

The fourth and final plank in our operational model has been added: When Scripture makes a pronouncement about generic man, there is a transcultural principle involved. However, this transcultural principle is necessarily expressed in some cultural context, so that we must distinguish between the principle and the manner in which it is expressed. The particular expression may or may not be critical to affirming the principle, but in any case there will likely be far more critical applications of the principle than its original expression.

Thus Paul wrestled with the implications of Christian faith for himself and the people of Corinth, not crudely with dogmatic assertions to bend them into submission, but expertly with sometimes subtle nuances of meaning. He reasoned that we must not compromise our distinctive as the people of God, that we ought to enjoy God's bounty to the full, that we should be sensitive to how our behavior affects others, and that we should be aware of how the principles of our particular calling can best be worked out in various cultural settings.

Now that we have explored our second biblical paradigm — Paul's admonition to the Corinthians — we are primed to investigate extrabiblical examples of the task of doing theology across cultures.

part three

Case Studies: Theoretical

5

The Yin-Yang Model
of Thought

We come now to critique a bold theological venture dealing with the nature of reality itself. The risk and potential in doing so are equally great. We risk compromising the Christian perspective on life but we sense the possibility of opening Oriental culture to the uninhibited spread of the gospel. We press on in the confidence of a high view of biblical authority and cultural integrity.[1]

Jung Young Lee notes that theologians are paying increasing attention to the yin-yang perspective. He concludes that "the growing interest in the use of the both/and [yin-yang] category of thinking by Western theologians will have a profound implication as an impetus for the creation of universal theology."[2] In this chapter we will briefly examine a cultural context (West Africa) whose religious orientation offers a ready access to Christian theology. We will then consider Lee's contention that the yin-yang perspective may be a similar bridge between Christianity and the Chinese world.

1. There is an abundance of case studies available; for example, Gerald H. Anderson and Thomas F. Stransky, eds., *Mission Trends No. 3: Third World Theologies* and *Mission Trends No. 4: Liberation Theologies in North America and Europe*; and C. Peter Wagner and Edward R. Dayton, eds., *Unreached Peoples '81.*

2. Jung Young Lee, "The Yin-Yang Way of Thinking," in *What Asian Christians Are Thinking*," ed. Douglas Elwood, p. 65.

The West African Experience

The *object* of theology is God and of Christian theology God as ultimately revealed in Christ. The *task* of Christian theology is to preserve a proper balance between the transcendence and immanence of God; the incarnation provides us with the means to do so.

The task of Christian theology has been relatively easy in a cultural context like West Africa. The nationals were as a rule henotheists, believing in a supreme being along with lesser gods. Many readily identified the Christian God with their high god and Christ as the immanent expression of that transcendent being. Their idols became superfluous as a result. The Christian faith easily took root in a compatible soil and its growth has been rapid.

Let us analyze what happened in the process. Karl Barth reminds us that "when we Christians speak of 'God,' we may and must be clear that this word signifies *a priori* the fundamentally Other, the fundamental deliverance from the whole world of man's seeking, conjecturing, illusion, imagining and speculating."[3] The West African concept removed the high god from the daily affairs of life. He could be approached only on especially critical occasions and then with uncertainty as to his response. He resembled what Barth calls the "fundamentally Other." This West African perspective was more compatible with genuine Christian faith than was the perspective of Barth's antagonists, who in spite of their profession to be Christians had excluded the priority of divine transcendence.

Missionaries in West Africa were not content to declare the transcendence of God, but went on to explain how He has been revealed in Christ (see John 1:18). God had called out a special people, and among that people He Himself appeared in order to bless in the fullness of time all the nations.

3. Karl Barth, *Dogmatics in Outline*, p. 36.

The experience of my friend Clement Idachaba illustrates the way Christian faith breaks through to the West African's consciousness. Clement's father was a traditional tribal priest and Clement often helped in preparing the sacrifice at the sacred tree. But one day he became inexplicably ill. All efforts failed and he continued to get worse. His father heard of an itinerant "man of God" in the district and solicited his help. This mysterious person was a servant of the high god, though he had never heard of Christ. He prayed for Clement and the lad soon recovered.

Clement dedicated himself to the high god. He reasoned that the high god had restored life to him and that he should offer his life in return. A short time thereafter he first heard the gospel and gladly responded. He had already turned his back on the sacred tree; now he trusted his future to Christ.

The Yin-Yang Perspective

The Orient presents a different kind of challenge than does West Africa. The ancient Chinese did in fact have a concept of the high god that closely resembles that of the West African, but it seems to have been obscured by subsequent religious developments. This high god was called "Shangti" — the Supreme Emperor, the Most High, the Only One.

Jung Young Lee's preference for the yin-yang perspective rather than Shangti is understandable. While the latter seems more compatible with Christian faith, the former is more central to Oriental thought as it has developed. Yin-yang is at the heart of the cultural orientation.

Lee's proposal ought to be weighed carefully, if for no other reason than that it offers an open door and warm welcome. If Christian theology can come this way, the possibility for success is great. The question before us is, Can we do Christian theology within the context of yin-yang thinking?

In brief, "yin-yang" is a term used in Chinese philosophy to indicate the two basic principles of the universe. Their "polarity sums up all life's basic oppositions, good-evil, active-passive, positive-negative, light-dark, summer-winter, male-female, etc. But though [these] principles are in tension, they are not flatly opposed. They complement and counter-balance each other."[4] The all-embracing circle (Figure 1) represents the final unity of Tao. Taken together the two principles are clearly monistic in character; reality is conceived of as a unified whole which functions by way of an inherent polarity of opposites.

Figure 1   Symbolic Representation of Yin-Yang

Lee argues that the yin-yang perspective may be employed for ultimate matters. With "the yin-yang way of thinking, it is no trouble at all to think that God is both *transcendent* and *immanent* at the same time."[5] It is true that, given this perspective, we would have no trouble in thinking of God as both transcendent and immanent; but it would be difficult to conceive of Him also as personal.

Lee is prepared to qualify theism in order to preserve his perspective. He concludes that "God, who transcends all categories, cannot be a personal God *only*. . . . To make God personal is to limit him."[6] This leads us back to the inclusive circle of the Tao and to monism. And we had best be certain

4. Huston Smith, *The Religions of Man*, p. 211.
5. Lee, "Yin-Yang," p. 66.
6. Ibid.

that we want to travel to this destination before buying a ticket on Lee's theological journey.

A Critique

We discover in Psalm 8 a perspective reflected throughout Scripture. The psalmist ponders, "What is man, that Thou dost take thought of him? And the son of man, that Thou dost care for him?" (v. 4). "Man's life is marked off, separated from both God and beast. His eyes sweep the heavens. Behind the work he senses a power. Behind the artistic order he perceives an architect."[7] Man also surveys the brute world about him, as one charged with superintending it. He walks in a peculiar twilight zone between the Creator and the remainder of the creation.

The psalmist's perspective is diagramed in Figure 2. God is distinct from His creation, as suggested by the solid line; man is differentiated from the remainder of creation, having been created to reflect God's image and to superintend the rest, as represented by the broken line.

God

Man

Extended Creation

Figure 2 The Psalmist's Perspective

The question now before us, simply put, is whether the yin-yang model is compatible with the psalmist's perspective. We judge that it is not, because yin-yang does not allow for the qualitative difference between God and the creation. On the other hand, the biblical point of view requires such a

7. Morris A. Inch, *Psychology in the Psalms*, p. 19.

distinction, as was pointed out in our first chapter concerning the concept of revelation.

However, there may be a more modest use for the yin-yang perspective, one which would provide a helpful bridge to Oriental thought. For instance, there is a striking polarity in the biblical concept of man. God formed man of the dust of the ground and breathed into him the breath of life. Biblical man is a peculiar product of earth and heaven. We cannot understand him simply in terms of one or the other; rather we must recognize that both earth and heaven are reflected in man.

The yin-yang perspective, then, can be used by Christians as an approach to the Oriental world. The problem is not with the perspective itself, but with carrying it too far. The yin-yang perspective is a reasonable way of looking at man's life (with allowance made for Shangti). But it fails in its conception of God, for it does not distinguish satisfactorily between God and creation.

There is a still more modest possibility for use of the yin-yang perspective, this time in reference to man and woman. Dietrich Bonhoeffer comments on their creation, "They are no longer without one another; they are one and yet two."[8] They are complementary like the yin-yang, one and yet two. This perspective might be of value not only for the East but for the West as well. It could go a long way in dealing with the current struggle with sex identity that seems to be reaching an epidemic stage.

It remains for us to present several propositions which will draw the loose ends of our discussion together:

1. The Shangti tradition seems much more compatible with Christian thinking than does the yin-yang perspective. We ought to make use of the former, if not as an alternative to the latter, at least as a needed corrective. This would point

8. Dietrich Bonhoeffer, *Creation and Fall* and *Temptation*, p. 60.

the Oriental audience to an earlier tradition, much in the way Paul directed the Athenians to some of their own poets (Acts 17:28).

2. The relationship between Shangti and yin-yang might be profitably explored to discover the best avenue for expressing the Christian faith. Consider, for instance, the case of Chuangtee, a recent Taoist who described the Tao as "the way of heaven."[9] In his thinking there is apparently a connection between Shangti and yin-yang, but the precise nature of the relationship and its usefulness are not immediately evident.

3. The temptation to promote the yin-yang perspective in such a way as to deny the qualitative distinction between God and the creation must be resisted at all cost. As we observed at the outset of this work, there is a vast gulf set between God and man, a gulf that resembles the endless expanse of the heavens.

4. There are more modest uses of the yin-yang perspective that might be considered. We mentioned two: (1) the conception of man as the product of heaven and earth and (2) the complementary nature of man and woman. Making use of the thought patterns of the local culture is in keeping with our earlier emphasis on the continuity between man's former experience and the Christian message.

5. There may be ideas now developing which will modify (or even replace) the thought patterns which have been dominant in the past (the Shangti tradition) and the present (the yin-yang perspective). Witness the global-city mentality that seems evident virtually everywhere one travels these days. It is at least possible that while Christians struggle to relate their faith to traditional but weakening patterns of thought, the future may pass them by.

9. James Pong, *Christian Doctrine and Chinese Religious Thought*, p. 1.

6

An Eastern Critique of the Western Concept of Man

Theological dialogue works both ways. The previous chapter was in effect a Western critique of Eastern thought. We turn now to an Eastern evaluation of a traditional Western concept of the nature of man. The Sinhalese Lynn de Silva, observing that "the biblical view of man is holistic, not dualistic,"[1] charges that the West has assumed uncritically a Greek dualism in its understanding of man's nature. This sets the stage for our present discussion.

The Greek Heritage

Oscar Cullmann has graphically described the Greek view of man which so deeply influences those of us in the West: "The soul, confined within the body, belongs to the eternal. As long as we live, our soul finds itself in a prison, that is, in a body essentially alien to it."[2] The soul is imprisoned within the body until such time as the soul may by death be set free. The dualism remains intact whether in life or death.

Cullmann compares the Greek perspective of man with that of Scripture. "Can there be a greater contrast than between Socrates and Jesus?" he asks. Socrates discourses serenely with his disciples as the moment of his death

1. Lynn de Silva, "The Problem of the Self in Buddhism and Christianity," in *What Asian Christians Are Thinking*, ed. Douglas Elwood, p. 110.
2. Oscar Cullmann, "Immortality of the Soul or Resurrection of the Dead," in *Immortality and Resurrection*, ed. Krister Stendahl, p. 13.

approaches, while Jesus "offered up both prayers and supplications with loud crying and tears to Him who was able to save Him from death" (Heb. 5:7). For Socrates this was the time for his soul to be released but for Jesus it was an encounter with man's "last enemy" (I Cor. 15:26).

Cullmann further notes the reaction of the emperor Marcus Aurelius to the way in which the Christian martyrs faced death. One might expect that this great Stoic leader would have been favorably impressed by their stalwart determination but this was not the case. The enthusiasm with which they met death displeased him: "The Stoic departed this life dispassionately; the Christian martyr on the other hand died with spirited passion for the cause of Christ, because he knew that by doing so he stood within a powerful redemptive process."[3] The Greek-trained mind had little understanding and even less appreciation of the biblical perspective of man. De Silva's appeal to recapture a scriptural point of view seems to be in order.

The Biblical Perspective

"The Hebrew idea of personality is that of an animated body, not (like the Greek) that of an incarnated soul."[4] We read that "the LORD God formed man of dust from the ground, and breathed into his nostrils the breath of life; and man became a living being" (Gen. 2:7). He was from the first viewed as an animated, living creature rather than as a soul inhabiting a body for a time.

The Hebrew could and did describe man in various ways but never so as to repudiate his conviction as to man's essential nature. The contrary was in fact the case: each new portrait of man further accented his basic character as a living creature.

Reflect upon Job as an example of biblical man. We dis-

3. Ibid., p. 46.
4. H. Wheeler Robinson, *The Christian Doctrine of Man*, p. 27.

cover him sitting among the ashes, potsherd in hand so that he could scrape his festering skin, repulsed by his condition, grieved by the loss of family and wealth, pondering the meaning of the disaster which had befallen him, and contending with his troublesome friends. He reflects all of the aspects of a sensate creature: he sees, hears, and smells. There is not the slightest hint of there being something unnatural in all this, as if his personality were trapped in flesh. Job *is* flesh.

Job courageously shares his feelings with his insensitive associates. He describes how it feels, having once enjoyed the earth's bounty, to be cast aside, forsaken, and suffering. His friends shield themselves from Job's emotions, wrapping themselves in self-righteousness, likely fearful that if they were to identify too closely with his situation, they might be the next to fall prey to his pitiable condition. But in all of this, the feelings they suppress and those that surface, they along with Job illustrate man's sentient nature.

The patriarch attempts to reason through his dilemma. He reaches back to his previous understanding for some clue, weighs the circumstances around him, and attempts to anticipate the future. He functions as a rational creature, but reason is no more a feature of his general nature than is his flesh or feelings. Biblical man, despite all his diversity, remains an integral unity.

Job ponders what course of action to take. He is not simply a creature acted upon, the product of eternal forces, but he can act and alter life as a result. The patriarch also admits that he is accountable for his behavior: his freedom must be exercised in a responsible fashion. This too is a feature of his life.

Job's repeated references to God alert us that, when pondering himself and his lot, he always keeps the Creator in mind. Recall that "God created man in His own image" to oversee the extended creation and to enjoy its benefits (Gen. 1:27–30). It is this special relationship (not the imprisonment of a soul in a body) that gives man his peculiar character.

De Silva rightly concludes that "the biblical view of man is holistic, not dualistic." We in the West have allowed the Greek dualism of soul and body to creep into our thinking and to usurp the biblical emphasis on man as a living creature or animated body. We need to be corrected.

It remains to be seen if de Silva's subsequent proposal is a good one. Solutions have a way of compounding the problem they seek to resolve. We ought to proceed with at least as much care as we have taken up to this point.

The Anatta Doctrine

De Silva introduces the *anatta* concept as "a corrective to the wrong notion that has invaded popular Christian thinking. Christian theology can be greatly enriched by the absorption of the *anatta* doctrine into its system of thought."[5] *Anatta* "means the existential awareness of one's nothingness, nullity or unsubstantial nature. The ethical impact of this awareness is the realization that there is no enduring reality within man corresponding to the notion of 'I,' 'me,' and 'mine' — a notion to which man tenaciously clings and which is thus the root cause of all evil."[6] De Silva further suggests that it was this root cause of evil that Jesus struck at when He announced, "If any one wishes to come after Me, let him deny himself, and take up his cross, and follow Me" (Matt. 16:24).

In critiquing de Silva's proposal, the first point to be noted is that while he introduces *anatta* as "a corrective to the wrong notion that has invaded popular Christian thinking," he himself has a wrong notion as to exactly what the biblical teaching is. *Anatta* is the repudiation of the notion that there is any real or persisting self. This is a far cry from Jesus' admonition that we deny ourselves in order to follow Him in the service of others. It is in fact the opposite. Jesus taught that we should love our neighbor as ourself; He did not intro-

5. De Silva, "Problem of the Self," p. 113.
6. Ibid., p. 108.

duce self-denial as a metaphysical dogma but as an ethical imperative.

Nor did Jesus understand the root cause of evil to be the affirmation of self. Instead, He represented the root problem as man's revolt against God. The accent on self is proper as long as it does not obscure God and others.

This is not to say that de Silva's argument is thoroughly without merit. There are elements of truth throughout. De Silva claims that the *anatta* concept can enrich Christian theology in three areas — the psychophysical, the ethical-social, and the transcendental. We will examine each of these in turn.

The first of the areas in which de Silva sees the *anatta* concept as enriching Christianity is the psychophysical. The *anatta* concept is presented as an effective remedy for Greek dualism. It is that, but it is such a radical cure that it threatens to kill the patient. The helpful ingredient in the proposed cure is that it reminds us of the transitoriness of life *as we now experience it.* Paul testifies that the perishable shall put on the imperishable and the mortal put on immortality (I Cor. 15:54). Indeed, we cannot hope to sustain the perishable, but neither ought we to deny the imperishable. Thus we ought to turn our attention from the temporal to the eternal and the result will be precisely what de Silva suggests — a dynamic quality of life, what one author has described as "living out our immortality."

The second area is the ethical-social. This application of the *anatta* concept at first seems more appealing than the one we have just examined, but it is not without serious difficulty. The problem is not, as de Silva claims, "the false notion of the self." It is rather the promotion of self to the exclusion of others. Authentic life consists of sharing together before God, receiving and giving in a reciprocal relationship. Although de Silva's premise is wrong, its application is nobler than the practical results of orthodox interpretations that fail to recognize the social dimension of man's nature and responsibility.

The final area is the transcendental. Here we seem to find the least difficulty with de Silva's approach. The *anatta* doctrine, with its emphasis on the bliss of transcending self, can be used as a bridge to presenting the biblical revelation. De Silva comments, "The more a person goes beyond himself, the more is the spiritual dimension of his life deepened, the more he becomes a true person."[7] Communion is the key: when we reach beyond ourselves to God, we also reach to the depths of our own being. We find ourselves in the pursuit of the Almighty.

It is only in the rarest instances that there is absolutely no element of truth in what we identify as error or no element of error in what we call truth. This is what we have attempted to illustrate in the current instance. The *anatta* doctrine imposes on Scripture something quite foreign, but it was constructed out of some valid observations, and these observations (rather than the doctrine in its refined form) offer possibilities for linkages with Christian theology.

An added word is in order regarding de Silva's proposed methodology, which he describes as interreligious and intercultural dialogue. Dialogue is fine if its purpose is correctly understood. It must not, however, lead to religious syncretism. It is this abuse of dialogue that we must guard ourselves against. We must dialogue from strength of conviction and in anticipation that it will enrich our understanding.

To restate some of our more critical conclusions concerning de Silva's proposal:

1. De Silva's criticism of the Western dualistic interpretation of man is well taken. The prevailing Western view fails to capture the holistic character of man as portrayed in Scripture. We need to take a longer look at the biblical text and let it shape our thinking.

7. Ibid., p. 114.

2. However, de Silva's appeal to the *anatta* doctrine as a corrective is suspect. It elevates the concept of self-denial to a metaphysical status; the substantial and continuing nature of personality is rejected. De Silva attempts to soften this effect on Christian belief but the result is not convincing. The *anatta* doctrine, as it has been refined in Buddhist thought, is simply on a collision course with the Christian concept of man.

3. Nevertheless, many of the perceptions which gave rise to the *anatta* doctrine are not as suspect. They may be explored with profit. In fact, they do not seem to violate the biblical teaching in the way that unqualified Hellenic dualism and Buddhist *anatta* do. They are, as a high view of culture suggests, a *reasonable* way of looking at things.

4. We are reminded, as a result of this discussion, that there can be some truth in error and that error continues to plague truth. We therefore need to reaffirm the often quoted maxim, "All truth is God's truth."

7

Liberation Theology

Liberation theology in its varied forms is perhaps the most prominent theological trend of our day. It is not our purpose to analyze the movement as a whole or the overall contribution of the author on whom we will focus (Gustavo Gutierrez). Nor shall we explore in detail the theological tradition from which he comes or the social context in which he operates. Only with such careful restraint can we hope to advance some pertinent comments regarding the topic at hand.

We are coming to the heart of the Christian faith when we consider the saving work of Christ. We are dealing with the historical fact of Christ's death and resurrection, its enactment on behalf of lost mankind, and its resolution of the dilemma of sin. We must be especially conscientious when we hone this message in a particular cultural setting.

Two Views of Salvation

Gustavo Gutierrez defines salvation as "the communion of men with God and the communion of men among themselves."[1] He is uneasy with the "quantitative" notion of salvation, which emphasizes the individual, ecclesiastical, and futuristic aspects of salvation. He concentrates instead on the "qualitative" notion of salvation, which stresses corporate, universal, and current dimensions.

1. Gustavo Gutierrez, *A Theology of Liberation*, pp. 151–52.

We must attempt to clarify this point. There is, on the one hand, the church secure in its role as the gate of heaven, dispensing sacraments and spinning fantasies concerning the life to come; and on the other, the church as God's bridgehead on enemy soil, preaching deliverance to the oppressed and sustaining man in his struggle against every form of tyranny. The former has too often been the posture of Christianity and our notion of salvation; the latter, Gutierrez hopes, will be the wave of the future.

Gutierrez at times seems to deny the former in order to stress the latter, but there are sufficient qualifying comments to suggest that this is not his intent. We simply note this problem in passing, realizing that his purpose is to advocate a more comprehensive view of salvation, one "which embraces all human reality, transforms it, and leads it to its fullness in Christ."[2]

The problem, as Gutierrez sees it, is that we have created a duality of history: sacred and secular. "Rather there is only one human destiny irreversibly assumed by Christ, the Lord of history. His redemptive work embraces all the dimensions of existence and brings them to their fullness."[3] Salvation is not marginal to the real life of man but at the heart of "the historical current of humanity." All of history must be viewed with reference to Christ's salvific action.

This in brief is the position taken by Gutierrez regarding the nature of salvation (we are disregarding some of his more extreme comments in favor of those which moderate his approach). There are numerous refinements, such as his comments on the levels of liberation,[4] but to explore these would likely obscure our discussion.

The Biblical Concept

The distressed Philippian jailor, prostrating himself before Paul and Silas, inquired of them, "Sirs, what must I do to be

2. Ibid., p. 151.
3. Ibid., p. 153.
4. Ibid., pp. 21–37.

saved?" (Acts 16:30). What did he mean by the question? He may not have had in mind the meaning which Paul and Silas attached to the word *saved* and which formed the basis for their reply, "Believe in the Lord Jesus, and you shall be saved, you and your household." He may simply have meant, "How may I escape from the penalty assessed for failure to keep prisoners chained?" or "How shall I be delivered from the wrath of the gods — as evidenced by the earthquake?"

Outside the biblical context "salvation" primarily related to recovery from an illness, but "it also referred to deliverance from every kind of calamity. In the New Testament the meaning is extended to signify total recovery and release from the disease of sin."[5] Scripture employs the word *salvation* (and its cognates) in all these ways. When the extended theological meaning is in view, Scripture associates with "salvation" terms like "atonement," "justification," "conversion," "regeneration," "sanctification," and "glorification." "Salvation," then, is no longer one word by itself but a term in association with others which flesh out its extended meaning.

Only when we grasp the nature of the extended meaning of "salvation," as developed by and through a variety of related concepts, can we appreciate the relevance of the response Paul and Silas made to the jailor. Only then can we understand why "Believe in the Lord Jesus" qualifies as the answer to "What must I do to be saved?"

We cannot pursue this topic further without some comment on what we are saved *from*. That is to say, we cannot get at the root meaning of salvation without understanding the nature of sin.

A good working definition of sin is "any lack of conformity to the will of God." This definition indicates that sin is at least primarily a religious concept. While it has certain implications for man with respect to himself and his relation to others, it basically concerns his relationship with the Almighty. It is any lack of conformity to the will of *God*.

5. Donald G. Bloesch, *The Christian Life and Salvation*, p. 40.

Sin also suggests that man falls short of what God intended that he should be. Paul declared that "all have sinned and fall short of the glory of God" (Rom. 3:23). Sin is any lack of conformity to the *will* of God.

Sin is both the failure and the reason for the failure. Man opts to abide by something other than God's gracious purpose; this is likely the emphasis Paul intended in the verse just quoted. Man prefers darkness to the light of God, the far country to the Father's home, his way to the way of God. Sin results from choice and not by chance.

Salvation is the process whereby man is returned to favor with God, to walk in communion with Him, and to fellowship with Him as kindred spirits. The various concepts associated with "salvation" help enlarge our understanding of the process, the means by which it is achieved, and the resulting consequences. An extended discussion of salvation would require that we explore these related matters but this is beyond the scope of our present endeavor.

However, there is one additional factor to consider before returning to Gutierrez's proposal. That is what theologians have sometimes called "salvation history": the particular events associated with redemption. Scripture announces that "God, after He spoke long ago to the fathers in the prophets in many portions and in many ways, in these last days has spoken to us in His Son" (Heb. 1:1–2). This special series of episodes, along with the interpretation given to them, constitutes salvation history.

Salvation in the context of salvation history is not, nor could it ever be, strictly a private matter. We become part of what some have described as God's people moving through history. We learn to pray to *our* Father and for *our* needs. We assume a common historical legacy and a shared responsibility to pass it on to others.

Our treatment of the biblical material has been exceedingly brief but it is sufficient to provide the needed background. We will now consider whether Gutierrez's theological position is compatible with the biblical material or whether it leads us astray.

An Appraisal of Gutierrez

In theology we must be concerned not only with what is said but with what is not said or deemphasized so that it receives little attention. The present instance is a case in point. In Gutierrez's position there are truths obscured to the degree that they are difficult to recognize, and wrong implications are drawn as a result.

We begin with the concept of sin. Gutierrez comments, "Insofar as it [sin] constitutes a break with God, sin is a historical reality, it is a breach of the communion of men with each other, it is a turning in of man on himself which manifests itself in a multifaceted withdrawal from others."[6] He does allow that sin is alienation from God, but he quickly steers our attention away to its societal effects.

Gutierrez advocates an "intensive" approach to sin, that is, dealing with it as a present reality. He downgrades the "extensive" approach, which concerns itself with the life beyond. But we ought to give proper consideration to both for they are actually one and the same thing. Biblical salvation is concerned not simply with the future life or the present but both.

When we think only of the future life, our stress falls on faith, to the exclusion of obedience. When we focus solely on the present, our emphasis changes to obedience, to the disregard of faith. All of this calls to mind Dietrich Bonhoeffer's often repeated words: "Only he who believes is obedient, and only he who is obedient believes."[7] We ought not to separate faith and obedience, nor the present and the future as they relate to salvation.

Salvation is more than temporal deliverance. It involves

6. Gutierrez, *Liberation*, p. 152.
7. Dietrich Bonhoeffer, *The Cost of Discipleship*, p. 69.

our reconciliation to God for eternity. It is both now and not yet. Christ has begun a work which we expect Him to complete in the future. Exclusive focus on either the now or the not yet must be tenaciously resisted as a distortion of biblical teaching.

Critiques of liberation theology have expended much of their energy on its bent toward violence as a legitimate avenue for social change, but violence is probably the result of a distorted view of the theological platform rather than an integral plank of the theological platform itself. Violence results from an unbalanced concentration on the present life, our immediate circumstances, and the alternatives currently available for use. It obscures the fact that God's judgment grinds inevitably but slowly through the course of history and toward a consummation.

The author has set forth his attitude toward violence in another connection.[8] There are basically four avenues to social change: revolution, reformation, revaluation, and regeneration. Revolution is a radical change of society through compulsion and violence. Reformation is gradual improvement of prevailing social patterns. Revaluation is a fresh perception of and new direction in social behavior. Regeneration is the renewal of individual lives by the Spirit of God. Revolution and regeneration are polar strategies, the other two falling somewhere in between.

We recall Jesus' warning, "All those who take up the sword shall perish by the sword" (Matt. 26:52). What is the problem with the revolutionary alternative? Revolution is, in one word, *excessive*. Its advocates presume they have knowledge significantly superior to that of their antagonists and/or the consent of the masses to use any means at their disposal in order to benefit all. They also assume that the deep wounds inflicted by violence can be successfully overcome. But "the

8. Morris A. Inch, *The Evangelical Challenge*, pp. 124–26.

new system provides neither panacea nor the promise of permanence. Our difficulties reincarnate in novel forms."[9]

Regeneration is the more promising of the two polar alternatives. It involves a commitment that transcends narrow, partisan causes and seeks the welfare of all. It motivates the individual, in league with others, to seek every man's good — as the Spirit of Christ seeks to express Himself through us. Regeneration also incorporates the important features of revaluation and reformation (and, in the more extreme instances, revolution as well). But violence is to be allowed with only the greatest of caution, for it can easily deceive us and thus mock our efforts, no matter how good our intention or with what willingness we are prepared to sacrifice.

There are, to be sure, liberation theologians who are reluctant to turn to violence but that is not the point. Their characteristic emphasis on the present and deemphasis of the future set up a virtually intolerable tension that courts violence. Or so it seems.

Gutierrez advocates a comprehensive view of salvation and well he should. But a comprehensive approach must include a healthy concern for both the now and the not yet. It is not clear that Gutierrez succeeds with respect to the latter.

A related comment on Gutierrez's theological methodology is in order here. He is prone to what I have come to label "rib-picking," cutting away the theological associations which flesh out the meaning of a given biblical teaching. In this case, he focuses on salvation practically without regard to the *ordo salutis*: those associated theological concepts mentioned earlier.

The problem with rib-picking is not simply that it loses the richness associated with a biblical truth but it encourages us to make substitutions for what is lacking. We read in associations from the social situation and endow them with biblical sanction. We become crusaders without a divine call-

9. Ibid., p. 125.

ing, baptize the unrepentant because of a mutual cause, and withdraw from Christian brothers who see the issue differently.

Be assured that this is no incidental matter. It can amount to preaching another gospel. We repeat Paul's warning, "As we have said before, so I say again now, if any man is preaching to you a gospel contrary to that which you received, let him be accursed" (Gal. 1:9).

Another facet of Gutierrez's position is his attack on the concept of salvation history, which he refuses to distinguish from history as a whole. But if everything is salvation history, then nothing is salvation history, and man as a whole remains alienated from God. Salvation history should be thought of as God's calling out a special people to bear His name. It is not evident how Gutierrez can sustain this particularism in his enthusiasm to describe all of history as redemptive.

It is time to tie together our critique of Gutierrez's position with our broader subject of doing theology in a cultural setting:

1. Gutierrez says that God is concerned for the oppressed, is active on their behalf, and calls us to join with Him in their struggle for deliverance. Gutierrez appeals for discontinuity between the Christian mission and the status quo which we have come to accept.

2. Gutierrez errs by disassociating the concept of salvation from the rich store of related vocabulary. He picks the theological rib clean before reconstructing the notion of salvation — which is, then, necessarily incomplete and potentially misleading.

3. Liberation theology's tendency toward violence gives us further concern. Does this suggest a failure to recognize a meaningful continuity between man's pre- and postsalvation experience? If so, we must urge again the importance of both continuity and discontinuity from a Christian perspective.

4. Gutierrez's proposal seems at best a needed theological corrective of a one-sided emphasis on the life to come, an

emphasis which tends to ignore our responsibility to ease the burden of the oppressed. But even when cast in the best possible light, his position presents no long-range view or adequate solution as it invites us to engage the present task. We need to balance our theological endeavor.

part four

Case Studies: Practical

Followers of Isa

Our case studies now take a turn away from theory and toward praxis. We are no doubt all familiar with the maxim, "What one does speaks more eloquently than what he says." Some years ago I was talking with a Jewish friend about the Holocaust. He protested some passing remarks made by Dietrich Bonhoeffer which had anti-Semitic overtones. I acknowledged the comments but also pointed out that Bonhoeffer had been personally instrumental in saving several Jews during the genocide. My friend was taken aback; after a brief pause, he concluded, "That is the real test of any man — demonstration of what he believes."

We ought therefore to approach the matter of praxis with all seriousness, not as some secondary issue but as the fleshing out of faith. The ultimate test of our theological endeavor is getting beyond (not away from) preachment to practice.

A New Approach to the Muslim World

The Muslim faith is not simply a religion but a way of life. It seeks to govern not only one's religious thinking but his social, political, and cultural activities as well. With little hope of changing the current of Muslim culture, the Christian who comes to such a situation must find a way to express his Christian convictions meaningfully in the cultural setting. Phil Parshall has faced this challenge; it is his pilgrimage in praxis we shall consider.

Through the story of Halim Ali, a nineteen-year-old dissatisfied with life, Parshall describes a traditional missionary approach to Muslims.[1] Living in a small bamboo hut with a large family, Halim spent long days plowing the family plot with a sickly ox. When Christian literature was left at the home, Halim responded with interest. He made his way to the mission compound, where he found a medical clinic, school, training center, and experimental farm. His own drab existence suffered by contrast.

Receiving food, shelter, and religious training at the compound, Halim became a Christian. When he told his family of his decision, their reaction was predictable and severe: he was "regarded as a traitor to family, friends, country, and religion." His options were to recant or flee.

Various perspectives are worth noting. "The *missionary* rejoices that a brand has been plucked from the flaming fire; the *home church* in the U.S.A. enthusiastically adopts the support of this courageous young man who has 'forsaken all' for his faith; the *villagers* symbolically bury an old pair of Halim's sandals in retribution against a despicable outcaste who dared to reject all societal norms and accepted a foreigner's religion where adherents eat filthy pig meat and worship three gods."

The results of such conventional methods have been meager and the procedure held up for question. Parshall and his associates have worked through an alternative approach with direction from a convert by the name of Simon. In two years with this alternative approach, thirty-seven Muslims, many of them family heads, responded to the claims of Christ. All remained in their villages, witnessing to Christ as accepted members of their families.

Parshall lists various adaptations which he and his associates have agreed to make to the cultural setting — six adap-

---

1. Phil Parshall, "Evangelizing Muslims: Are There Ways?" *Christianity Today*, 5 January 1979, p. 30. His thought is more thoroughly expounded in *New Paths in Muslim Evangelism: Evangelical Approaches to Contextualization.*

tations in lifestyle and eighteen in worship practices.[2] Among the adaptations in lifestyle: (1) the missionaries wear clothing similar to that of the villagers; (2) many of the missionary men grow full beards; (3) Muslim dietary practices are adopted (e.g., no pork). Among the adaptations in worship practices: (1) a facility for washing prior to prayer is provided outside the worship center; (2) believers remove their shoes and sit on the floor during prayer times; (3) Bibles are placed on folding stands such as are used for the Koran in the mosques; (4) prayer is offered Muslim-style — with uplifted hands and often with eyes closed; (5) chanting of the attributes of God, the Lord's Prayer, and personal testimonies is encouraged; (6) worshipers embrace in Muslim fashion; (7) no particular emphasis is placed on Sunday (seeing that the Muslim considers Friday the holiest day); (8) the name "Followers of Isa" (Jesus) is used in order to avoid the negative connotations of the word *Christian*; (9) churches are organized much like the loose-knit structure of the mosque. Those who are not of Muslim cultural background are welcome to worship but expected to adopt the prevailing practices. These practices result in breaking the ghetto complex traditionally associated with missions to Muslims. Thus the Christian faith is introduced as a catalyst into the prevailing Muslim culture.

A Critique

For present purposes we must resist the temptation to wander off in an attempt to determine what is the proper Christian attitude toward non-Christian religions in general and the Muslim faith in particular, except as this may have direct bearing on the issue of a Christian's adapting to a Muslim culture. We earlier opted for a high view of Scripture, as the authoritative revelation of God to man, rather than as simply the insights of religious men somehow sponsored by God. This gives the Bible a unique place among the other

2. Parshall, *New Paths*, pp. 25–26; cf. "Evangelizing Muslims," p. 31.

great religious classics, such as the Koran. It is not one of a number but one of a kind.

By making both the study of Scripture and worship based on the Scripture central aspects of the new congregations, Parshall's innovative approach gives the Bible a unique place. The Bible replaces the Koran as the focus of the convert's thinking and expression; this is reinforced by placing the Bible on wooden stands like those used to hold the Koran in mosques.

We note in passing that the Koran takes considerable liberty with the biblical text and its teaching, and that whatever is stated in the Koran is for the orthodox Muslim a settled truth. Thus the faithful are advised, "He who has denied a verse of the Koran, it is allowed to behead him."[3] To say that transferring one's allegiance from the Koran to the Bible under such circumstances is a sensitive issue is, then, a classic understatement.

Of course one cannot hope to follow Jesus and fail to study His teaching as recorded in Holy Writ. Apparently what Parshall is attempting is not a simple exchange of one book for the other, but, as the self-designation of "Followers of Isa" implies, a discipleship process that introduces the Scripture into its rightful place. The study of Scripture will help erase faulty stereotypes, for example, the notion that the Christian believes in three gods. Scripture will demonstrate that the "Followers of Isa" are genuinely monotheists.

Is there a danger of syncretism here? We are reminded of the prophets' and apostles' uncompromising attack on religious syncretism. Willem Visser 't Hooft distinguishes four great syncretistic waves with which the people of God have had to contend: the ancient idolatry which earned the prophets' ire, the Hellenic influence that plagued the early church, the response to the Enlightenment, and the current trend

3. John A. Hardon, *Religions of the World*, vol. 2, p. 100.

(which he allows may simply be an extension of the third).[4] In light of Visser 't Hooft's portrait of the struggle against religious syncretism, how are we to view adaptations to the Muslim way of life? There seems to be no easy answer to this question, but we should keep in mind that while Islam is a corruption of Christian teaching, it can also be used to help correct Christian practice.

Islam is a corruption of Christian teaching. It begins with a misunderstanding of Christian doctrines, reinforces the false impression by way of the Koran, and rejects Christianity in the same fashion. Obviously some correction is called for from a Christian point of view. The convert may think of Mohammed as the means through which his attention was drawn to Isa, but now that he has discovered Isa, Mohammed must decrease in importance. With others of like precious faith the convert will come to affirm that Jesus is Lord.

Though a corruption of Christian teaching, Islam can be used to help correct Christian practice — particularly through its uncompromising emphasis on the transcendent character of God. It calls into question not only the use of icons and relics, but also the cultic adoration of charismatic leaders and uncritical acceptance of popular ideas of success. The faith modeled by congregations of persons raised in the Muslim religion will be worthy of careful note by the church at large.

While these converts must be careful not to compromise their faith in the living God, as revealed in and by Isa, they do have a fullness of life which can be affirmed with thanksgiving. Parshall's suggestions for adaptation of various Muslim forms are permeated with a sense of celebration. They encourage the convert to appreciate life as a gift of God which can be recognized in ways proper to the cultural setting.

In addition, the adaptation of various Muslim forms displays a concern about not offending others. This can be observed primarily in the various concessions missionaries

4. Willem Visser 't Hooft, *No Other Name*, pp. 12–35.

have made to the Muslim way of life, for example, placing no special emphasis on Sunday, manifesting a humble attitude divested of the Western feeling of superiority, wearing traditional dress, renting homes and adopting a lifestyle as simple as one can without injury to physical and emotional health.[5]

All of these considerations parallel Paul's instruction to the church at Corinth concerning the eating of meat offered to idols. A direct similarity to Corinth can be seen in the wearing of the veil in modern Muslim villages, and there the missionary women have at least on occasion assumed the practice. This cultural similarity could be used as a springboard to exploration of other aspects of the sex roles.

The propriety of any given adaptation will require continuing review. We sometimes discover a serious mistake which is difficult to correct once it has become part of the developing tradition. Where an existing practice is adopted, care must be taken that it is understood within the new framework of faith. Thus, although fasting is encouraged, it must be understood that fasting in itself does not provide merit or lead to acceptance by God.

It is no doubt significant that Parshall's innovative approach follows to a large degree the insights of a national. Simon had entered into fraternal dialogue with the missionaries in order to devise a strategy. Thus the best way for Christians to approach the Muslim community was delineated with the help of someone who was rooted in the cultural context.

Now that we have made our way through the case study, it is time to sum up:

1. Basic to Parshall's approach is the idea that converts from Islam should call themselves "Followers of Isa." The term *Christian* has come to have a decidedly derogatory connotation. The Koran teaches, "Take not the Jews or Christians

5. Parshall, "Evangelizing Muslims," p. 31.

for friends. They are but one another's friends. If any of you takes them for his friends he is surely one of them. Allah does not guide evildoers."[6] The change in designation is at least an effort to circumvent the history of mutual antagonism between Muslims and Christians, and to bring attention back to Isa. While this runs the risk of losing much of the Christian legacy as represented in the history of the church, it offers a fresh and possibly creative approach.

2. The other adaptations in form which Parshall suggests flow more or less naturally from the change in designation and from the ideal of establishing a homogeneous church of Muslim converts. The question arises, How is this distinctive church to be related to the church at large, and in particular to the traditional church already established in Muslim countries? Parshall's answer is, as we have observed, that the traditional Christian is welcome to worship but at the same time is expected to adjust to the practices of the Muslim-convert church. This is not fully satisfactory although alternatives do not readily come to mind. Perhaps this is simply another instance of the tension we must live with in affirming high views of both the Bible and culture. If so, while the traditional Christian must take care to maintain a high view of culture, the innovative Christian (as understood by Parshall) must take care not to lose his high view of Scripture.

3. Parshall's proposal illustrates the importance of role models. One missionary has suggested that it takes three generations to bring about a well-rounded Christianity. We learn as we observe others, individually and collectively; much of the Christian faith is caught in this fashion. Obviously, the missionary who takes on cultural customs is no substitute for even a first-generation national convert. Nevertheless, by making certain adaptations to the culture the missionary can give the whole process a start.

4. We conclude with a statement of the purpose underlying

6. Surah 5.51.

Parshall's endeavor: "As far as possible, all peripheral barriers to Muslims becoming Christians are to be removed. If there are obstacles to faith, let it be in the area of theological confrontation."[7] That is to say, "Our purpose is to think through our Christian faith in a prevailingly Muslim culture." However we word it, the task before us is to discover and sustain some areas of continuity between the Christian faith and the particular cultural context with which we are dealing.

7. Parshall, "Evangelizing Muslims," p. 31.

9

Honor Your Father and Mother

In discussing Chinese religion Lewis Hopfe observes: "Historically it is the aged father, mother, grandfather, or grandmother who dominates the Chinese home. It is the obligation of the children to support the elderly, to obey them, and to give them proper burial after their death. Even after the parents' death the child is obligated to maintain their grave site, to remember them and their deeds, and to offer sacrifices to them. Western students of Chinese life have often referred to this attitude as 'ancestor worship.' "[1] Once this practice has been identified as ancestor worship, the Chinese Christian is caught in a bind between his faith and his culture. On the one hand, he must reserve his worship for God alone, and on the other, custom expects from him a filial piety expressed by a determined set of practices.

This chapter considers the resolution proposed by Lim Guek Eng in an unpublished paper entitled "Christianity Versus Ancestor Worship in Taiwan." She has in turn drawn significantly from an aged pastor named Cho, who has had a highly successful ministry with rural folk deeply involved in ancestor worship.

A Functional Substitute for Ancestor Worship

After an insightful discussion Eng concludes with some proposals for "an adequate functional substitute for new Tai-

1. Lewis M. Hopfe, *Religions of the World*, p. 164.

wanese converts who have a background in ancestor worship." These proposals have to do with ancestral tablets, Christian memorials, and traditions associated with grave sites. We shall consider each of these in turn.

"In the Chinese mind, it is believed that ancestor spirits live in the 'other world' as much as they [lived] while on earth. Hence they must be fed, cared for and propitiated. If these needs are not met the ancestors will be hungry and dissatisfied and in a sense, they will become malevolent spirits who roam around and cause trouble, disease and calamities, upon the family as well as the neighbourhood. Thus in order to avoid such dangers, the family of the deceased sets up a tablet on the table of the family altar which symbolizes the articulation of the spirit with the human world."[2] The Christian convert who has in the past been deeply immersed in this way of thinking often experiences fear and anxiety at the thought of removing the ancestral tablet from its prominent place in the home.

In some rural homes in mainland China the portraits of Communist leaders have replaced the traditional ancestral tablet. Eng makes an analogous suggestion: "Rather than leaving [the spot where the ancestral tablet was set up] empty, a tablet of approximately the same size may be put in place of it. This latter tablet has a design with the symbol of the Cross right in the middle, probably a picture of Jesus' praying in the Garden of Gethsemane, and Bible verses fitting the sides of the tablet."[3] She proposes such verses as, "Believe in the Lord Jesus, and you shall be saved, you and your household" (Acts 16:31), and "But as for me and my house, we will serve the LORD" (Josh. 24:15). In the place where the names of ancestors were originally inscribed might be, "Honor your father and mother . . . that it may be well with you, and

---

2. Lim Guek Eng, "Christianity Versus Ancestor Worship in Taiwan," p. 2.
3. Ibid., pp. 14–15.

that you may live long on the earth" (Eph. 6:2–3; cf. Exod. 20:12; Deut. 5:16).

In addition, Eng suggests that family prayer meetings be held once a week, at first under the guidance of the pastor. Leadership can be shifted to the head of the house (father or grandfather) after he has gained sufficient knowledge of the Scripture and its applications. This will serve not only in the initial period after conversion but as a regular ongoing practice for the family.

Ancestral temples (halls) are relatively recent additions to ancestor worship in Taiwan. They are used by the family clan for annual rites of ancestor worship and for communal feasts which reflect background and economic situation. These activities promote the clan's internal unity and cooperation against pressures from outside.

Eng proposes construction of Christian memorials according to Chinese architectural forms "in order to serve the need when large segments of the rural village are won to Christ. The memorial may be used to conduct memorial services at the time of death, during All Souls' Day, the Chinese New Year [which is the day when the folk people have traditionally remembered their dead], and other occasions, such as birthdays."[4] She adds that this will provide an opportunity to emphasize the convert's new religious identity in Christ and the role of the Holy Spirit in fostering a deeper cohesiveness and concern among the people.

In addition there are various practices associated with the tomb. We recall in this connection Hopfe's observation that "even after the parents' death the child is obligated to maintain their grave site, to remember them and their deeds, and to offer sacrifices to them." Eng sees the possibility of turning these traditions away from narrow concern with one's own lineage to the wider perspective of the household of God — what she calls "God's forever family." She quotes Galatians

4. Ibid., p. 15.

6:10: "While we have opportunity, let us do good to all men, and especially to those who are of the household of the faith." Thus the ideal of filial piety is broadened to include the family of faith.

All of this implies both a privilege and a responsibility. Eng sees the responsibility primarily in terms of the task of evangelism but obviously the idea could be extended in many directions. Like ancestral tablets and temples, practices associated with the tomb provide opportunity for instruction and growth in the Christian faith.

An Evaluation

We have already noted that Donald McGavran estimates that all but 5 percent of the cultural components in Nagaland have been automatically embraced by the Christian faith (p. 20). The remainder fall into three categories: "Some components Christianity welcomes as particularly wholesome and desirable. Some Christianity changes and improves. And, on the authority of the Bible, Christianity declares that a few components are unacceptable to God and must be abandoned."[5] There are examples of all three categories in the Chinese practice of ancestor worship.

What in the area of ancestor worship does Christianity welcome so as to celebrate its presence, extend its priority, and make provision for its continuance? Most obvious is the element of filial piety, that is, respect of one's elders. Eng describes filial piety as "the hallmark of Chinese society"; it is no less a hallmark of biblical teaching.

For instance, note Jesus' response when He was asked by the Pharisees and scribes, "Why do Your disciples not walk according to the tradition of the elders, but eat their bread with impure hands?" (Mark 7:5):

5. Donald A. McGavran, *The Clash Between Christianity and Cultures*, pp. 39–40.

> You nicely set aside the commandment of God in order to keep your tradition. For Moses said, "Honor your father and your mother"; and, "He who speaks evil of father or mother, let him be put to death"; but you say, "If a man says to his father or his mother, anything of mine you might have been helped by is Corban (that is to say, given to God)," you no longer permit him to do anything for his father or his mother; thus invalidating the word of God by your tradition which you have handed down; and you do many such things like that. [vv. 9–13]

It appears that the custom allowed children to pledge their goods to the temple (whether they actually contributed them or not) and thus escape any obligation to care for their parents. Jesus condemned this practice as a flagrant breach of filial piety.

The Western Christian who is fortunate enough to visit the Chinese culture will feel there a stronger sense of filial piety than he has experienced in his own culture. In China the elderly are cared for within the family circle instead of being rushed off to a convalescent home at the first sign that they might become a burden.

Closely related to filial piety is the concept of filial obedience. We honor our parents by being obedient to their wishes; we dishonor them by disregarding their wishes. Consider the case of the fellow whose mother used to say to him, "When I want your opinion, I'll tell you what it is." Although we may enjoy a good laugh at his expense, her comment prompts us to consider the sobering truth of just how far we in the West have strayed from the ideal of filial obedience. The traditional Chinese culture differs substantially from the West in this regard and thus stands closer to the Bible teaching.

Filial piety and obedience often carry over in terms of respect to the elderly as a whole. In some cultures all of the elderly men will be addressed as father or grandfather and the elderly women as mother or grandmother. Though expressed differently from culture to culture, this respect for the elderly is an aspect of culture which is highly compatible with the biblical perspective.

McGavran's second category of cultural components not automatically embraced by the Christian faith consists of those which "Christianity changes and improves." All three of Eng's suggestions fall into this category: a replacement for the ancestral tablet, Christian memorials in place of ancestral temples, and appropriate adaptation of practices associated with the tomb. We agree with the idea of providing a substitute for the ancestral tablet; this is far better than leaving the tablet where it is or allowing the revered spot to stand empty. Simply leaving the tablet would continue the old associations with the spirits and ancestor worship. Allowing the space to remain empty, on the other hand, would break the line of continuity with the past and forfeit the favorable connotations of the ancestral tablet, particularly those related to filial piety.

As to the detail of the replacement, perhaps the ancestral lineage could be included, much the way we in the West keep pictures of our parents and grandparents in the living room. In fact, one might construct a visual component, perhaps including multigenerational photographs. With the passage of time after the initial conversion in the family, all of this would become more meaningful from a Christian point of view — the faithful service of Christian ancestors could be recounted on particular occasions.

The suggestion that we replace the traditional ancestral temple with a Christian memorial touches on a familiar practice in Scripture. For instance, Joshua instructed the people to select twelve stones from the middle of the Jordan to be a perpetual sign among them. "Let this be a sign among you, so that when your children ask later, saying, 'What do these stones mean to you?' then you shall say to them, 'Because the waters of the Jordan were cut off before the ark of the covenant of the LORD; when it crossed the Jordan, the waters of the Jordan were cut off' " (Josh. 4:6–7). The stones were to be a memorial to the mighty acts of God.

The Christian memorial can likewise serve as a reminder of the mighty acts of God on behalf of His people, in redeeming them, sustaining them, and enabling them to minister to others. When the children inquire, "What does this memorial signify?" the elders can recount the many things which God has done on their behalf and on behalf of those who went before them.

Of course, preservation of some of the traditional practices associated with the grave site is in no way to be regarded as an attempt to provide material needs to the dead. Rather, in adapting some of the traditions we are to view the godly lives of those who have died as a continuing example and encouragement as we press on in the Christian life. Placing memorial flowers on the grave is but a token of our life commitment to the Christian heritage we have received from them.

Preserving some of the old traditions at the tomb is also a pledge to be of service and especially to see that the faith we have received from our ancestors shall not die with us. We promise before God and such witnesses as stand with us to pass on the godly heritage to others.

We come now to those cultural components which are unacceptable and must be rejected. There seem to be two primary elements involved: worship of one's ancestors per se and fellowship with the spirits. The Christian reserves his worship for God alone. One's ancestors may not presume on the divine prerogative of worship, nor would it be coveted by the Christian forebear.

All of the traditional rituals are interrelated with belief in the spirits. The beneficial spirits are generally referred to as *Shen* and the evil spirits as *Kwei*. "Generally the common people performed sacrifices and rituals that would put them on good terms with the Shen and keep them safe from the

Kwei."[6] But Christ became the mediator of all that is good (although we do not mean to reject the idea of ministering angels) and the deliverer from evil forces. Thus the traditional notion of intercourse with the spirits must be set aside.

To weave together the loose ends of our discussion:

1. We see in this case study the importance of distinguishing carefully the precise meaning of individual words. The idea of ancestor *worship* is offensive to the Christian, but that of parental *respect* is readily acceptable. The problem seems to be that in traditional Chinese culture the notions of worship and respect are blended together, so that the Christian must be sure to distinguish them. If he does not, he will either render to his ancestors that which must be reserved for God alone or he will think himself impious for failing to render due consideration to his ancestors.

2. Once the concepts of worship and respect have been properly distinguished, the latter may be changed and improved by the influx of the Christian faith. The goal is that the Christian community become a model of filial piety for the rest of society.

3. But this goal will not be achieved if the wisdom of the past is rejected. Traditional Chinese culture, especially as relates to the Confucian classics, remains a veritable storehouse of riches. The Chinese Christian is not to be the product of his culture alone or his faith alone, but of his faith as it is fleshed out in cultural form.

4. In our earlier discussion concerning the veiling of women we saw that a principle can be variously expressed from culture to culture (p. 40). Here we have a similar instance, this one dealing not with sex roles, but with the parent-child relationship. The biblical principle of obedience, generated out of honor, is clearly set forth (Eph. 6:1–3), as is the reciprocal duty of the father (Eph. 6:4), but precisely what honor

6. Hopfe, *Religions*, p. 163.

entails differs from one culture to another. For instance, looking into the eyes of an elder in Yoruba culture would be disrespectful but failing to do so in Western culture might be thought of as an effort at deceit.

5. With Paul's instruction to the church at Corinth in mind, a final observation should be made concerning sensitivity to others. After a period of time, the convert should be better able to distinguish between what is legitimate practice as reconceived within his Christian faith and what must be surrendered as incompatible with it. At the same time he must be considerate of those of his circle who are still in a transition stage as well as those who are not making the transition with him, who see things only from the former perspective. He must not allow the liberty he has found in Christ to snuff out the first glimmer of faith in another.

part five

Summary

10

Christian Transformation of Culture

We turn now to the question of how the Christian faith alters culture. This will provide an opportunity to recall some of the ground we have covered, as well as help us to focus on the concern at hand. Implicit throughout is the call to set one's faith in his cultural context.[1]

The Church as Catalyst

We hold the church to be God's catalyst for transforming culture through the impact of the gospel. Jesus taught His disciples, "You are the salt of the earth," and again, "You are the light of the world" (Matt. 5:13–14). They were to let their "light shine before men in such a way that they may see your good works, and glorify your Father who is in heaven" (v. 16). This seems to suggest that culture is a beneficiary of the Christian presence.

And indeed, culture is a beneficiary of the Christian presence — but only in a derivative sense. Karl Barth reminds us that "the subject of dogmatics is the Christian Church."[2] It

1. This topic is variously touched on in works such as Tetsunao Yamamori and Charles R. Taber, eds., *Christopaganism or Indigenous Christianity?*; David J. Hesselgrave, *Communicating Christ Cross-Culturally*; idem, *Planting Churches Cross-Culturally*; idem, ed., *New Horizons in World Mission: Evangelicals and the Christian Mission in the 1980s*; J. Herbert Kane, *Christian Missions in Biblical Perspective*; and Gerald H. Anderson, ed., *Asian Voices in Christian Theology*.
2. Karl Barth, *The Humanity of God*, p. 9.

is only the Christian fellowship which has experienced the redeeming power of God, celebrates the victory of Christ, and seeks to serve as empowered by the Holy Spirit. It is in the church that we sense God at work, so that even the counsel of hell cannot prevail against it (cf. Matt. 16:18).

How is God working with the church? First, by calling it out as the people of God. The Scripture teaches that it is "a chosen race, a royal priesthood, a holy nation, a people for God's own possession" (I Peter 2:9). As such, the church is to call attention not to itself but to the One who shows mercy to confessed sinners. It is a signpost to direct the prodigal home to a loving Father. It is like a former beggar who tells others where they may find the bread of life.

There is another side to the church as a witnessing community, in that it exhibits the fruit of the Spirit: love flowing out into joy, peace, patience, kindness, goodness, faithfulness, gentleness, and self-control (Gal. 5:22–23). It portrays, although imperfectly, the compassion of God for those who flee His grace. It bears the reproach of the world, returning good for evil, in hope that men will see the error of their way and turn to the living Lord.

But it is not enough for the church to come apart as the people of God and simply stand there as a witness to Him. The church is also commanded to go out serving in Christ's name. Lesslie Newbigin observes that "it is never enough for the Church simply to be there and to say 'Come.' There has to be a movement of *kenosis*; one has to be willing to go, to become simply the unrecognized servant of men where they are, in order that *there*, perhaps in quite new forms, the authentic substance of the new life in Christ may take shape and become viable."[3] We can speak of this as a rhythm, a double movement of coming and going in the life of the church—the church answers the invitation to come apart as the people of God and then goes out into the world to serve.

3. Lesslie Newbigin, *Honest Religion for Secular Man*, p. 121.

Here we recall our earlier discussion concerning liberation theology. The problem with that approach as far as it relates to the present topic is that it fails to give proper recognition to the central role of the church in God's redemptive strategy. It compromises the gospel out of humanitarian concern for the oppressed, and loses the needed leverage provided by the community of faith. All such efforts to bypass the church, no matter how well-meaning, are doomed.

How does the church impact on culture? Primarily by being the church, in response to the invitation to come apart and the charge to go. The church affects culture simply by virtue of being the body of which Christ is the head. As Paul reminds us, God "put all things in subjection under His feet, and gave Him as head over all things to the church, which is His body, the fulness of Him who fills all in all" (Eph. 1:22–23).

The Means of Impact

The question of how faith impacts on culture involves not only the Christian community but what T. S. Eliot designates as "the community of Christians," that is, a Christian consensus that helps set cultural norms. Eliot explains, "It will be their identity of belief and aspiration, their background of a common system of education and a common culture, which will enable them to influence and be influenced by each other, and collectively to form the conscious mind and the conscience of the nation."[4]

Here we concern ourselves with the broad reaches of the humanities: philosophy, literature, music, art, and the like. We seek to permeate the world with a Christian perspective. We do not suppose that as a result any culture will become genuinely Christian in an absolute sense, but each culture is more or less susceptible to a Christian point of view faithfully advanced.

Eliot identifies two stages in the development of what he

4. T. S. Eliot, *Christianity and Culture*, p. 34.

calls "the community of Christians": interaction among Christians and their collective impact on others. Responsibility for applying faith to cultural setting falls mainly on the national Christian. One way in which he ought to proceed is to participate in dialogue with Christians from other cultures (Eliot's first stage). This explains why we have considered such an array of topics as the yin-yang way of thinking, liberation theology, and ancestor worship. A reverse case in point is the Eastern critique of classical Western anthropology (chapter 6), which likewise illustrates the primary role of the national Christian in dialogue with Christians from other cultures.

The national Christian ought also to proceed by way of dialogue with other nationals (Eliot's second stage). He does not talk *at* but rather *with* his fellow nationals about the Christian convictions he holds. He impacts culture from within, as one who respects the integrity of his culture and cherishes it as a vehicle through which the gospel may be expressed. Just as dialogue with Christians from other cultures helps to clarify the nature of Christian conviction, so dialogue with non-Christian nationals helps to preserve cultural integrity. Both together will assist the national Christian in focusing his faith in his cultural setting.

Eliot adds to the concepts of Christian community and community of Christians the idea of a Christian state. He conceives of the Christian state "as the Christian Society under the aspect of legislation, public administration, legal tradition, and form."[5] Like the community of Christians it is a Christian consensus, specifically, a consensus which influences the political realm — the passage of laws, the administration of justice, the establishment of legal precedents, and legal procedure.

Werner Elert argues that "the place to oppose evil is always within the political structure — not from the outside. The

5. Ibid., p. 21.

opportunity for such opposition is extremely limited in some political systems, but the mere appearance of an outstanding personality of unquestioned authority, the slightest manifestation of the will to be decent and just, is always an encouragement to the timid and a threat to the demons which forces them to retreat."[6] The question is not whether Christianity has a political influence, but how its influence can be employed wisely and effectively.

Elert suggests that there is a range of political influence available to the church. At one end is simple example: the mere appearance of a respected individual standing for that which he holds to be right is an encouragement to others. We find the force of sanction at the other end of the continuum: in between example and sanction there is a place for persuasion.

Phil Parshall and his associates have had to confront political realities. The Muslim political establishment revealed little inclination toward change. So the first step of Parshall and his associates was to take a stand *within* the political structure rather than to try to operate from outside. There they affirmed everything in the cultural context that seemed good and opposed what appeared unfavorable. And they participated in ongoing dialogue within the fellowship of believers and with those outside the fellowship. This is the process through which Christian influence builds.

How does the Christian faith impact on culture? Eliot has suggested that cultural and political realms will appropriate the Christian faith to varying degrees. Each of the entities Eliot discusses — the Christian state, the Christian community, and the community of Christians — has its own particular degree of influence on the realm in which it operates. "Among the men of state, you would have, as a minimum, conscious conformity of behavior. In the Christian Community that they rule, the Christian faith would be ingrained,

6. Werner Elert, *The Christian Ethos*, p. 121.

but it requires, as a minimum, only a largely unconscious behavior; and it is only from the much smaller number of conscious human beings, the Community of Christians, that one would expect a conscious Christian life on its highest level."[7] The church lies at the center, where it fosters conscious commitment to the cause of Christ, and extends its influence into cultural and political realms.

We are accustomed to thinking that someone either is a Christian or he is not; this is, of course, a valid way of thinking. But the way in which Christianity spreads its influence in the realms of politics and culture is better visualized by analogy with the incoming tide that washes over the shore and then retreats before making a further incursion. Christian influence surges and retires. At the point of high tide it seems to sweep everything before it, but at low tide it appears too feeble to do more than lap at the cultural and political shoreline.

Another Approach

We cannot begin to exhaust the possible ways of analyzing how Christianity transforms culture. However, we will take one more approach to the subject in order to help clarify the issues involved.

Each of us exercises responsibility in various settings. Some we assume voluntarily, others are determined for us. I am a son, brother, husband, father, citizen, faculty member, church member, member of professional societies, and ever so many other associations. I have certain obligations in each of these capacities. But there is for me as a Christian a loyalty to Christ that runs through all of these roles, helping me set priorities, perform faithfully, and sustain a positive attitude. I am in each of these areas a servant to Christ and therefore a servant like Christ.

As these areas of responsibility seem to coalesce in Christ,

7. Eliot, *Christianity and Culture*, p. 23.

the distinctions we have so carefully tried to make between the community of Christians, the Christian community, and the Christian state seem to blur together. This is as it ought to be, because the distinctions were made merely for the purpose of analysis. In making such distinctions we must be sure not to lose sight of the holistic nature of life. The Christian is inevitably *in* the world, even though we may correctly argue that he is not *of* it.

Everyone is required to serve in the areas of his calling: if he is a son, he must be a good son; as a citizen, he must be a good citizen. In each of these areas he must model the Christian faith for others to see and witness to his faith that they might hear. In this way Christianity can transform culture. There is for the Christian no escape from responsibility thus conceived. When he finds it difficult to fulfil his responsibility, he should ask for grace to be found faithful.

In this connection we mention again the high regard we have placed on Scripture as the authoritative Word of God. For it calls us to our place of service and sustains us as we attempt to serve. We are reminded that "all Scripture is inspired by God and profitable for teaching, for reproof, for correction, for training in righteousness; that the man of God may be adequate, equipped for every good work" (II Tim. 3:16–17).

Our high regard of Scripture calls to mind once again our high regard of culture as well. How are the two to interrelate, especially as regards the position of the national Christian? He has heard God's Word in his own cultural setting, and it is there he must decide whether or not to follow God's leading. It is the individual's decision, as Charles Hodge reminds us: "The obligations to faith and obedience are personal. Every man is responsible for his religious faith and moral conduct. He cannot transfer that responsibility to others; nor can others assume it in his stead."[8] Hodge reasons further

8. Charles Hodge, *Systematic Theology*, vol. 1, p. 184.

that if every man must answer for himself, then "he must judge for himself" how the Word of God bears on life within his cultural context.

The decision to follow Christ inevitably makes demands on the disciple. "At one point or another, in every culture, the sensitive Christian is brought up against the inescapable dilemma created by the conflict between culture patterns and his own relationship to God."[9] Jesus warned, "If anyone comes to Me, and does not hate his own father and mother and wife and children and brothers and sisters, yes, and even his own life [by comparison with his love for Christ], he cannot be My disciple" (Luke 14:26).

The demands are heavy but this is because the task is so great. God means to regenerate men and through them individually and collectively to transform culture as well. The task will never be complete for those who strive to be faithful in the interim before the Lord's return, but they are encouraged to believe that their labors are not in vain in the Lord (I Cor. 15:58).

9. William A. Smalley, ed., *Readings in Missionary Anthropology*, p. 249.

Bibliography

Altizer, Thomas J. J., ed. *Toward a New Christianity: Readings in the Death of God Theology*. New York: Harcourt, Brace and World, 1967.

Anderson, Gerald H., ed. *Asian Voices in Christian Theology*. Maryknoll, NY: Orbis, 1976.

_____, and Stransky, Thomas F., eds. *Mission Trends No. 3: Third World Theologies*. Grand Rapids: Eerdmans, 1976.

_____. *Mission Trends No. 4: Liberation Theologies in North America and Europe*. Grand Rapids: Eerdmans, 1978.

Barth, Karl. *Dogmatics in Outline*. New York: Harper and Row, 1959.

_____. *The Humanity of God*. Richmond: John Knox, 1960.

Berger, Peter L., and Luckmann, Thomas. *The Social Construction of Reality*. Garden City, NY: Doubleday, 1967.

Bloesch, Donald G. *The Christian Life and Salvation*. Grand Rapids: Eerdmans, 1967.

Bonhoeffer, Dietrich. *Christology*. London: Collins, 1966.

_____. *The Cost of Discipleship*. New York: Macmillan, 1963.

_____. *Creation and Fall* and *Temptation*. New York: Macmillan, 1959.

_____. *Ethics*. New York: Macmillan, 1955.

Brunner, Emil. *Christianity and Civilization*. London: Nisbet, 1948.

Cullmann, Oscar. "Immortality of the Soul or Resurrection of the Dead." In *Immortality and Resurrection*, edited by Krister Stendahl, pp. 9-53. New York: Macmillan, 1965.

De Silva, Lynn. "The Problem of the Self in Buddhism and Christianity." In *What Asian Christians Are Thinking*, edited by Douglas Elwood, pp. 105-18. Quezon City: New Day, 1978.

Elert, Werner. *The Christian Ethos*. Translated by Carl J. Schindler. Philadelphia: Fortress, 1957.

Eliot, T. S. *Christianity and Culture*. New York: Harcourt, Brace and World, 1949.

Elwood, Douglas, ed. *What Asian Christians Are Thinking*. Quezon City: New Day, 1978.

Eng, Lim Guek. "Christianity Versus Ancestor Worship in Taiwan" (unpublished paper).

Gutierrez, Gustavo. *A Theology of Liberation*. Translated by Caridad Inda, Sr., and John Eagleson. Maryknoll, NY: Orbis, 1971.

Hamilton, Kenneth. *Words and the Word*. Grand Rapids: Eerdmans, 1971.

Hammond, T. C. *In Understanding Be Men*. Downers Grove, IL: Inter-Varsity, 1968.

Hardon, John A. *Religions of the World*. 2 vols. Garden City, NY: Doubleday, 1968.

Hesselgrave, David J. *Communicating Christ Cross-Culturally*. Grand Rapids: Zondervan, 1978.

———. *Planting Churches Cross-Culturally*. Grand Rapids: Baker, 1980.

———, ed. *New Horizons in World Mission: Evangelicals and the Christian Mission in the 1980s*. Grand Rapids: Baker, 1979.

Hodge, Charles. *Systematic Theology*. 3 vols. Grand Rapids: Eerdmans, 1946.

Hopfe, Lewis M. *Religions of the World*. Encino, CA: Glencoe, 1976.

Inch, Morris A. *The Evangelical Challenge*. Philadelphia: Westminster, 1978.

———. *Psychology in the Psalms*. Waco, TX: Word, 1969.

Kane, J. Herbert. *Christian Missions in Biblical Perspective*. Grand Rapids: Baker, 1976.

Kato, Byang H. *Theological Pitfalls in Africa*. Kisumu, Kenya: Evangel, 1975.

Kraft, Charles. *Christianity in Culture*. Maryknoll, NY: Orbis, 1979.

Lee, Jung Young. "The Yin-Yang Way of Thinking." In *What Asian Christians Are Thinking*, edited by Douglas Elwood, pp. 59–67. Quezon City: New Day, 1978.

Let the Earth Hear His Voice. Edited by J. D. Douglas. Minneapolis: World Wide, 1975.

Lewis, C. S. *The Screwtape Letters*. London: Collins, 1942.

McGavran, Donald A. *The Clash Between Christianity and Cultures*. Washington: Canon, 1974.

Machen, J. Gresham. *Christianity and Liberalism*. Grand Rapids: Eerdmans, 1923.

Mayers, Marvin K. *Christianity Confronts Culture*. Grand Rapids: Zondervan, 1973.

Newbigin, Lesslie. *Honest Religion for Secular Man*. Philadelphia: Westminster, 1966.

Nicholls, Bruce. *Contextualization: A Theology of Gospel and Culture*. Downers Grove, IL: Inter-Varsity, 1979.

Parshall, Phil. "Evangelizing Muslims: Are There Ways?" *Christianity Today*, 5 January 1979, pp. 30–31.

———. *New Paths in Muslim Evangelism: Evangelical Approaches to Contextualization*. Grand Rapids: Baker, 1980.

Pong, James. *Christian Doctrine and Chinese Religious Thought*. Taipei: Taiwan Diocesan, 1979.

Prayers: Ancient and Modern. New York: Doubleday, 1897.

Rackham, R. B. *The Acts of the Apostles*. London: Methuen, 1901.

Robinson, H. Wheeler. *The Christian Doctrine of Man.* Edinburgh: Clark, 1947.

Shaw, R. D. *The Pauline Epistle.* Edinburgh: Clark, 1903.

Smalley, William A., ed. *Readings in Missionary Anthropology.* Tarrytown, NY: Practical Anthropology, 1967.

Smith, Huston. *The Religions of Man.* New York: Harper and Row, 1958.

Stendahl, Krister, ed. *Immortality and Resurrection.* New York: Macmillan, 1965.

Stott, John. *Basic Christianity.* Grand Rapids: Eerdmans, 1958.

Thielicke, Helmut. *I Believe: The Christian's Creed.* Translated by H. George Anderson. Philadelphia: Fortress, 1968.

Visser 't Hooft, Willem. *No Other Name.* Philadelphia: Westminster, 1963.

Wagner, C. Peter, and Dayton, Edward R., eds. *Unreached Peoples '81.* Elgin, IL: David C. Cook, 1981.

Yamamori, Tetsunao, and Taber, Charles R., eds. *Christopaganism or Indigenous Christianity?* South Pasadena, CA: William Carey, 1975.

Subject Index

Scripture Index